You are about to start on an adventure that will reward you for the rest of your life . . .

If you find yourself in a situation where you seem to be going nowhere, or you feel inadequate and unable to face life with enthusiasm and confidence, ***this book is for you.*** If you are disgusted with mediocrity and not content to just drift through life, these pages offer you an alternative.

If you can make yourself open and receptive to new concepts, values, and beliefs, you will discover how you can systematically reorganize your thought processes to **awaken the new you!**

It makes no difference who you are, what you do, or what your life situation is. **You *can* achieve total self-confidence.**

—Dr. Robert Anthony

Berkley Books by Dr. Robert Anthony

HOW TO MAKE A FORTUNE FROM PUBLIC SPEAKING:
PUT YOUR MONEY WHERE YOUR MOUTH IS

THINK

THINK AGAIN

THINK ON

THINK AND WIN

THINK TOGETHER

THINK BIG

THE ULTIMATE SECRETS OF TOTAL SELF-CONFIDENCE

DR. ROBERT ANTHONY'S ADVANCED FORMULA
FOR TOTAL SUCCESS

DR. ROBERT ANTHONY'S MAGIC POWER
OF SUPER PERSUASION

50 IDEAS THAT CAN CHANGE YOUR LIFE!

DOING WHAT YOU LOVE, LOVING WHAT YOU DO

HOW TO MAKE THE IMPOSSIBLE *POSSIBLE*

THE
Ultimate Secrets
OF TOTAL
Self-Confidence

Dr. Robert Anthony

BERKLEY BOOKS, NEW YORK

THE BERKLEY PUBLISHING GROUP
Published by the Penguin Group
Penguin Group (USA) Inc.
375 Hudson Street, New York, New York 10014, USA
Penguin Group (Canada), 90 Eglinton Avenue East, Suite 700, Toronto, Ontario M4P 2Y3, Canada
(a division of Pearson Penguin Canada Inc.)
Penguin Books Ltd., 80 Strand, London WC2R 0RL, England
Penguin Group Ireland, 25 St. Stephen's Green, Dublin 2, Ireland (a division of Penguin Books Ltd.)
Penguin Group (Australia), 250 Camberwell Road, Camberwell, Victoria 3124, Australia
(a division of Pearson Australia Group Pty. Ltd.)
Penguin Books India Pvt. Ltd., 11 Community Centre, Panchsheel Park, New Delhi—110 017, India
Penguin Group (NZ), 67 Apollo Drive, Rosedale, North Shore 0632, New Zealand
(a division of Pearson New Zealand Ltd.)
Penguin Books (South Africa) (Pty.) Ltd., 24 Sturdee Avenue, Rosebank, Johannesburg 2196, South Africa

Penguin Books Ltd., Registered Offices: 80 Strand, London WC2R 0RL, England

The publisher does not have any control over and does not assume any responsibility for any author or third-party websites or their content.

A Berkley Book / published by arrangement with New Thought Publications

PRINTING HISTORY
New Thought edition published 1979
Berkley mass-market edition / September 1984
First Berkley trade edition / June 2006
Second Berkley trade edition / January 2008

Berkley trade paperback ISBN: 978-0-425-22189-1

The Library of Congress has catalogued the original Berkley trade edition as follows:

Anthony, Robert.
   The ultimate secrets of total self-confidence / Robert Anthony.
      p. cm.
   Originally published: San Diego, Calif. : New Thought Publications, 1979.
   ISBN 0-425-20975-X
   1. Self-confidence.   2. Self-actualization (Psychology)   3. Success—Religious aspects.
I. Title.   II. Title: Total self-confidence.

   BF575.S39A58 2006
   152.4—dc22   2005057165

PRINTED IN THE UNITED STATES OF AMERICA

10 9 8 7 6 5 4 3 2 1

Acknowledgments

No author ever writes a book alone. I have drawn the ideas from many sources including, of course, my own experiences in lecture work and private practice. People in the field of psychology, religion, and metaphysics have assisted me. Many prefer to remain anonymous, content with the fact that their knowledge and experience may help someone gain spiritual and psychological freedom.

It would be difficult to acknowledge everyone from whom I have borrowed ideas but I insist on thanking a few by name. I have been profoundly influenced by Anthony Norvell, my personal teacher and counselor; Marguerite and Willard Beecher for their excellent work in helping others to develop self-reliance; Lilburn Barksdale for his outstanding program and booklets on self-esteem; and the writings of Maxwell Maltz, Joseph Murphy, Emmet Fox, Abraham Maslow, Ralph Waldo Emerson, Napoleon Hill, and Ernest Holmes.

—DR. ROBERT ANTHONY

Dedication

To every person who wishes to improve the quality of his or her life, I acknowledge you for taking the time to buy and read this book. The time and effort sets you apart from the majority. As you become aware of your unlimited possibilities for creation you will not only prosper and develop yourself but you will gain a great wealth of information that will allow you to help others who can follow your example.

Contents

INTRODUCTION   *xv*
    The Unhappy Majority
    The Sheep State of Mind
    The Power to Change
    Fulfilling Your Needs First
    Come Aboard! It's Take-Off Time!
    21 Days Can Make a Difference

1. DEHYPNOTIZING YOURSELF   *1*
    How Your Beliefs Imprison You
    We Are Limited by Our "Mistaken Certainties"
    No One Likes to Change Their Present Level of Awareness
    Your Number One Priority
    Why You Can Change

2. BONDAGE OR LIBERTY?   *13*
    Self-Reliance
    Recognizing and Breaking the Dependency Habit
    Overcoming the Need to Manipulate
    The Fatal Decision of Conformity
    How Comparison Breeds Fear
    Competition—Killer of Creativity

Praise vs. Recognition
Freeing Yourself from Others

3. THE ART OF SELF-ACCEPTANCE   29
In the Beginning
The Major Addictions of a Person with Low Self-Esteem
The Most Common Emotional, Physical, and
        Psychological Characteristics of Low Self-Esteem

4. THE PROBLEM OF AWARENESS   41
You Always Do Your Best
Accepting Reality
The Destructive Power of Value-Judging
Understanding Your Motivation
How to Motivate Yourself Positively
Taking Responsibility
The Hold of Habit
You Cannot Give Up Anything You Regard as Desirable
Positive Habit Conditioning Program

5. I'M NOT GUILTY, YOU'RE NOT GUILTY   57
A Look at Morality
The Seven Major Forms of Guilt
Guilt Always Brings Punishment
Learning from the Past
Remember—You Always Do Your Best
You Are Not Your Actions
Make a Guilt Diary

6. THE POSITIVE POWER OF LOVE   *69*

Stop Looking for Others to Love You!

Doing Unto Others

Some Important Aspects of Love and Their
    Relationship to Your Individual Progress

7. MIND—YOUR OWN BUSINESS   *79*

You, Incorporated

The Law of Mental Magnetism

The Superconscious Phase of Mind Power

Great People Have Used This Power

Creative Power Channeled Through Desire

8. THE GOLDEN KEY OF CREATIVE IMAGINATION   *91*

Imagination Controls the World

The Conscious Phase of Mind Power

Waking Up Your Genie

The Correct Thinking Process

Facts You Should Know About Your Subconscious Mind

How to Program Your Genie

The Subconscious—A Creative Automatic Mechanism

You Already Have It

9. CHOOSING YOUR DESTINATION   *105*

What Will You Have?

Get the Writing Habit

Set Goals in the Six Major Areas of Your Life

Direct Action Worksheet

Give Yourself a Five-Year Plan for Growth

Start Where You Are
Not How Much But How Well
Getting Your Perspective
You Are Where You Want to Be
Respond to Life with Action
Fortune Favors the Bold
Making Friends with Failure
The Law of Expectancy
The Secrecy Principle

10. YOU DESERVE A BREAK TODAY   **125**
What is the Purpose of Meditation?
When to Meditate
Where Should One Meditate?
Before You Start
Meditation is a Three-Step Process

11. THE TIME OF YOUR LIFE   **135**
Is Time the Problem . . . Or Are You?
Every Journey Begins with the First Step
The "After Theory"
Don't Let Time Manage You—Manage It!
Time Becomes a Tool, Not a Tyrant
There Never Was a Better Time—For You

12. OVERCOMING FEAR AND WORRY   **145**
Reverse, Not Rehearse, Your Failures
Change, the Order of the Universe
Change Comes with Being Different

13. MOVE AHEAD THROUGH POSITIVE COMMUNICATION *153*

Listen! Listen! Listen!

We Are More Interested in Ourselves Than Anyone Else

Hold Only Positive Conversations

Use Plain Language

Let the Other Person Know They Are Impressing You

Give Sincere Recognition

Wait Until the Conversation Gets Around to You

Actions Speak Louder Than Words

Be on Time for Appointments

Remember People's Names

How to Meet People and Get to Know Them

Learn the Art of Small Talk

Get the Smile Habit

Be Careful of the Company You Keep

**14. ACHIEVING TOTAL SELF-CONFIDENCE THROUGH A
POSITIVE MENTAL ATTITUDE**   *173*

Positive Statements Release Creative Power

Move Ahead with These Affirmative Thoughts

Concentrate on What's Right with You

The New You

ABOUT THE AUTHOR   *179*

INTRODUCTION

THE UNHAPPY MAJORITY

As you look around at your fellow human beings, you will find it hard to ignore the fact that very few people are happy, fulfilled, and leading purposeful lives. Most of them seem unable to cope with their problems and the circumstances of daily living. The majority, settling for the average, have resigned themselves to "just getting by."

Resignation to mediocrity has become a way of life. As a result, feelings of inadequacy cause people, quite humanly, to blame society, other people, circumstances, and surrounding conditions for their failures and disappointments. The idea that people and things control their lives is so thoroughly ingrained in their thinking that they normally will not respond to logical arguments that prove otherwise.

William James, the eminent philosopher and psychologist, once observed that, "The greatest discovery of our age has been that we, by changing the inner aspects of our thinking, can change the outer aspects of our lives." Wrapped up in this brief statement is the dynamic truth that we are *not victims, but co-creators* in the building of our lives and the world around us. Or, as another sage puts it, "We aren't what we think we are, but what *we think,* we are!"

THE SHEEP STATE OF MIND

A lesson that has taken us far too long to learn is that the opposite of bravery is not cowardliness, but rather conformity. You may have spent valuable, irreplaceable years trying to fit into the parade only to learn, too late, that you will never fit in.

What makes us follow each other like sheep? It is because we are trying to conform to the majority. It's time to break out of this sheep state of mind and stop punishing ourselves because we are different from our family and friends, or anyone else for that matter. Much of our suffering can be eliminated if we refuse to let our lives be marred by conformity.

To *think* that our lives are controlled *in any way* by another individual, group, or society imposes a condition of mental slavery that makes us prisoners by our own decrees.

Our thoughts become the blueprints that attract from our subconscious minds all the elements that go into fulfilling our concepts, whether they be positive or negative. What we have in our lives right now is the outward manifestation of what has been going on in our minds. We have literally *attracted* everything that has come into our lives, good or bad, happy or sad, success or failure. This includes all facets of our experience, including business, marriage, health, or personal affairs.

Think about it! Your surroundings, your environment, and

your world all outwardly picture what you think about inwardly. By discovering *why you are the way you are,* you also find *the key to being what you want to be.*

THE POWER TO CHANGE

Shakespeare said, "We know what we are, but not what we may be."

Does this describe you? Do you concentrate on your limitations, your failures, your blundering way of doing things, seldom stopping to think of what you might be? The problem is that you have been conditioned since childhood by false concepts, values, and beliefs that have prevented you from realizing how truly capable and unique you are.

By virtue of your role as co-creator of your life, you have the power to change any of its aspects. Every great teacher has come to the same conclusion: *You cannot look to someone outside yourself to solve your problems.* As the Master Teacher reminded us so often, "The Kingdom of Heaven is *within.*" It is not in some distant land, and it is not up in the sky. Buddha came to the same realization when he said, "Be a lamp unto your own feet and do not seek *outside yourself.*" Self-healing powers are within. Health, happiness, abundance, and peace of mind are *natural* states of being once you break the bonds of negative thinking.

Unless you perceive your own true worth as a person, you cannot come close to achieving total self-confidence. Only to the degree that you can truly acknowledge your own unique importance will you be able to free yourself from self-imposed limitations.

Yes, I said *self-imposed*! Our parents, our family, our boss or society didn't do it to us. We do it to ourselves by *allowing* others to control our life.

Unless you get rid of your guilty feelings and cease belittling yourself for your imagined inadequacies, you will be one of those people who continue the fruitless struggle to attain total self-confidence and personal freedom. In order to be truly free, compassionate, warm, and loving, you must first begin by understanding and loving yourself. You have been told to "Love thy neighbor as thyself," but until you have a full appreciation of who and what *you* are, it defrauds both you and your neighbor!

FULFILLING YOUR NEEDS FIRST

One of the principal requisites for change and for a self-confident personality is to satisfy your own needs first. On the surface this may appear selfish, but let's remind ourselves that only when we have done our best to make the most of ourselves can we be of greatest service to our families, friends, co-workers, communities, etc.

Many people use the philosophy of service to others first as an escape from taking responsibility for changing their own lives. They say that their husbands or wives must come first; their boyfriends or girlfriends; their churches, families, or the world must come first. This is nothing but self-deception. An example of this kind of behavior is the person who buries himself sacrificially in a commendable project with missionary zeal when, in truth, he can't face and eliminate his own problems.

You can't change the world, but you *can* change *yourself*.

The only way the human situation will improve is for each individual to take charge of his or her own life. The time has come for you to stop everything else and give total priority to your needs first. This is the only way you will ever be free. Physical slavery is a punishable crime, but far worse is mental slavery, for the punishment is, as Descartes put it so well, "A life of quiet desperation."

COME ABOARD! IT'S TAKE-OFF TIME!

You are about to start on an adventure that will reward you for the rest of your life. You are going to learn new ways to break the bonds of limitation that have been holding you back.

If you find yourself in a situation where you seem to be going nowhere, or you feel inadequate and unable to face life with enthusiasm and confidence, this book is for you. If you are disgusted with mediocrity, disappointed by past results, and not content to just drift through life, these pages offer you an alternative. If you will allow yourself to be open and receptive to new concepts, values, and beliefs, you will discover why you should and how you can systematically reorganize your thought processes to awaken *THE NEW YOU*.

Once you master these principles, you will have more happiness, more love, more freedom, more money, and more self-confidence than you ever thought possible. Nothing is more rewarding in life than releasing your unlimited potential and leading a creative, purposeful life. It makes no difference who you are, what you do, or what your life situation is, *YOU* can achieve total self-confidence. And the approach is not nearly as difficult as you might think!

21 DAYS CAN MAKE A DIFFERENCE

Let's slip backstage for a moment and steal a glimpse at a simple but very effective learning technique. It's called THE 21-DAY HABIT.

It has been determined that it takes approximately twenty-one days to break an old, destructive habit or form a new, positive habit. It will take you at least that long to fully absorb the material in this book. Make no mistake. You will *understand* it immediately, but intellectual understanding alone is not enough to make the necessary changes. The real thrill comes when, at last, you KNOW it.

You must go from initial understanding to *knowing*. In order to *know* something, it must become a part of your thinking, feeling, actions, and reactions. And this takes time. So don't make the mistake of just reading the book once and saying, "I know it!" You won't "know it" until it has been absorbed into your consciousness and becomes a new habit pattern.

Put everything aside for a while and apply your full concentration to what you are reading. The hours spent in changing your negative, self-defeating habit patterns to positive, constructive ones will be a small investment compared to the rewards of a lifetime of accomplishment and freedom.

If at times I speak forcefully it is to cut through the heavy layers of mental resistance and reach a place within you where you already "know." A place where truth is recognized and heard. When this happens, there will be a feeling of heightened aliveness as something within you says, "Yes, I do know this is true."

To obtain the best results, read this book through once and familiarize yourself with the entire scope of the material. Then return to the specific chapters that are most meaningful to you. Let the principles sink deeply into your consciousness and, most importantly, ACT upon them without delay.

Now, if you are ready, let's get going!

THE

Ultimate Secrets

OF TOTAL

Self-Confidence

Dehypnotizing Yourself

Every person has been hypnotized to some degree either by ideas he has accepted from others or ideas he has convinced himself are true. These ideas have exactly the same effect upon his behavior as those implanted into the mind of a hypnotic subject by a hypnotist.

Over the years I have hypnotized hundreds of people to demonstrate the power of suggestion and imagination. To best illustrate my point, let me explain what happens when a person is hypnotized.

Under hypnosis, I tell a normal, healthy woman that she cannot lift a pencil that I have placed on a table. And, surprisingly, she finds herself unable to perform this simple act. It is not a question of her not *trying* to lift the pencil. She will struggle and strain, much to the audience's amusement, but she simply cannot lift the pencil. On the one hand, she is trying to perform the action through voluntary effort and the use of her body muscles. But on the other hand, the suggestion that "you cannot lift the pencil" causes her mind to *believe* that it is *impossible*. Here we find a physical force being neutralized by a mental force. It is a case of will power versus imagination. When this happens, *imagination always wins out!*

Many people think they can change their lives through sheer willpower. This is not true. Negative ideas in the imagination cause such persons to defeat themselves. Regardless of how hard they try, it's no use. They have accepted a false belief as if it were fact. All their ability, good intentions, effort, and will-power are of no avail against the powerful false belief they have accepted as truth.

In the same manner, I quickly prove that there is no limit to what a person can or cannot do when he or she is hypnotized because the power of imagination is limitless. To observers, I appear to have magical power to make her able and willing to do things she could not or would not ordinarily do. The truth is, of course, that the power is inherent in the subject. Without realizing it, my subject hypnotized *herself* into believing that she could or could not do these things. *No one can be involuntarily hypnotized, as each person collaborates in the hypnotizing process.* The hypnotist is only a guide who helps the subject ac-celerate the phenomenon.

I have introduced this simple demonstration of hypnosis to illustrate a psychological principle that can be of great value to you. This same principle is becoming increasingly evident in the modern educational process where the student, in effect, actu-ally educates himself with the skilled assistance of the teacher and, even more dramatically, in the healing arts where the pa-tient heals his own body under the professional guidance of a qualified healing arts practitioner.

Once a person *believes* that something is true (whether it is true or not), he then *acts* as if it were. He will instinctively seek to collect facts to support the belief no matter how false they may be. No one will be able to convince him otherwise unless, through personal experience or study, he is ready to change. Hence, it is easy to see that, if one accepts something that is *not* true, *all subsequent actions and reactions will be based upon a false belief.*

This is not a new idea. Since the beginning of time, both men and women have been in a kind of hypnotic sleep of which they were unaware, but which has been recognized by great teachers and thinkers throughout the centuries. These people have perceived that humankind limits itself through its "mistaken certainties" and have sought to awaken us to our potential for greatness, which goes far beyond anything we can possibly imagine.

It is, therefore, of utmost importance that *you do not assume you are awake to the truth about yourself.* Said another way, *you must not assume that what you now hold as truth is, in fact, really the Truth.* Instead, you must proceed with the idea that you are presently hypnotized by false beliefs, concepts, and values that are keeping you from expressing your true potential.

It may be astutely observed at this point that you and I are primarily the result of what we have been told and taught, and what we have been sold and have bought.

The average person never comes near reaching his unlimited potential because he is living under the false assumption that he already *knows* the truth. He believes what his parents have told him, what his teachers have taught him, what he has read, and what his religion has told him *WITHOUT ACTUALLY PROVING IT FOR HIMSELF.*

Millions upon millions of people have blindly followed the

rhetoric of so-called "knowledgeable" people without making sure that the principles these "experts" expound stand up to the realities of life. They further limit themselves by holding on to these concepts, values, and beliefs even after they have actually evolved beyond them. Fortunately, something or someone has triggered *your* interest in moving beyond your present level of awareness, which includes the discovery and development of total self-confidence.

Your first job is to *awaken* from the hypnotic condition that is presently keeping you from being the person you want to be. Read the following statement:

The degree to which you awaken will be in direct proportion to the amount of Truth you can accept about yourself.

Now read it again! This is the key that determines how much you will be able to change your life. In the words of the Master Teacher, "Know the Truth and the Truth shall set you free."

Many of the concepts presented in this book will be in direct opposition to what you now hold as the Truth. Some may even seem "way out" or illogical and will challenge your belief system. You will have a choice to either find out if they are true, or resist them. The choice is yours. This brings us back to what we said earlier: *Your life will be transformed in direct relation to the amount of truth you can accept about yourself.*

If you are sincere about changing your life and increasing your self-confidence, you must have an open mind. I neither want nor expect you to accept as true anything you read in this book, just because I say it's true. If you do, you will gain little from what you are reading. You must try out the principles for yourself. The inner conviction and security, which comes from having proved *to your own satisfaction* that what is presented as the Truth is indeed really the Truth, is the foundation upon which to begin building a dynamic self-confident personality.

In order to construct a new "functional" building on a site where a "nonfunctional" building exists, you first have to raze the old structure. This must be done by shattering those "mistaken certainties" that have held you back from expressing the unlimited, abundant, wholesome life you desire. This is primarily what this book is about.

HOW YOUR BELIEFS IMPRISON YOU

Just what are beliefs? They are the conscious and unconscious information that we have accepted as true. Unfortunately, our beliefs often imprison us and deny us access to what is real. A filter of misconceptions prohibits Truth's passage and we see only what we want, and reject everything else.

Truth can never be revealed to the so-called "firm believer." You know the type: always quoting "facts." He does not want to recognize anything outside of his belief and sees everything with which he disagrees as a threat. He goes through life labeling all that is new, different, and enlightening as "evil," or at least "unacceptable," and all that is old, traditional, and suppressing as "good." He cannot understand that Truth—no matter how painful—is always by its very nature "good," and that a lie—regardless of how much we are in love with it—is always by its very nature "bad."

To protect his beliefs, he builds a wall around his world. Some "firm believers" have a big wall and some a small one but, regardless of the size of the structure, it can only serve to shut out more of the Truth than it can hold.

The person who is a "firm believer" has no option to change his mind. This makes him ignorant. He can only recognize what lies *within* the walls he has built around himself and is prevented from exploring the limitless Truth, which lies outside the wall. What he fails to realize is that *Truth is always greater than any structure built to contain it.*

Belief and faith are not the same thing and should not be confused. Unlike belief, faith is not totally limiting. It recognizes there is more to discover and know, and that one must always seek to unfold more and more of the Truth. With faith, *all things are possible.* The "firm believer" always thinks he knows the answer. The person with faith, aware that there is always more to learn about him- or herself, constantly seeks enlightenment.

WE ARE LIMITED BY OUR "MISTAKEN CERTAINTIES"

If we wish to make a fundamental change in our life, we must first understand the root of our problems. This invariably lies in our "mistaken certainties."

Mistaken certainties are things we are sure are true but which, in fact, are not. They are generally based on *wishful thinking*, which distorts reality and leads to self-deception. We want things to be as we would *like* them to be rather than as they *are*. We look at the world through the filter of our beliefs, which blinds us to what is *real*.

We can only change the world to the extent that we can change ourselves. We can only change ourselves to the degree that we become aware of our mistaken certainties. Most of our troubles arise from expectations that have not become realities. Most of our disappointments come from our mistaken ideal of how we think the world *should be*, and what we think we "should" or "ought" to *do*, *be*, or *have*. This is known as *resisting* reality.

Emerson said, "We are what we think about all day long." Everything that is happening to you right now in your mental, physical, emotional, and spiritual world is the result of what is going on in your mind. To put it more exactly:

You accept, relate, or reject EVERYTHING in your mental and physical environment based on your PRESENT level of AWARENESS.

Your present level of awareness is determined by your education, environment, family life, childhood experiences, successes, failures, and religious beliefs.

You will discover that many of the things you thought were true are the things that, in reality, are *not true*. These will include the beliefs that make up the solid foundation of what you *assume* is reality. As you progress through this book, you will discover that everything you are accepting, relating, or rejecting is based on your present level of awareness. Unfortunately, your present level of awareness *may be faulty or distorted*.

NO ONE LIKES TO CHANGE THEIR PRESENT LEVEL OF AWARENESS

We find it difficult to change our present level of awareness because:

1. What we are picturing and imagining in our minds is based on what we now believe is the Truth, regardless of how faulty or distorted it may be. Our minds control our actions and reactions.

2. It is easier to give excuses or, as we prefer to call them, "logical reasons" why it isn't necessary, or even possible, to change.

3. We seek only those experiences that support our present values and avoid, resist, or, if necessary, forcibly reject those that are inconsistent with our existing beliefs.

4. We have built and programmed into our subconscious minds and central nervous systems the wrong responses to life situations that cause us to respond the way we have been programmed. In other words, we respond to the way we have been conditioned to FEEL and ACT. This "system" is of our *own creation* and only we can change its basic patterns.

Intellectually, we may agree that there are things in our life that we should change, but we almost always feel that our situation is different from everyone else's. This causes us to avoid, resist, and, if necessary, forcibly reject any idea that threatens our beliefs. Take, for example, the alcoholic. From his viewpoint of life, it seems rational to continue drinking. The drug user, the compulsive gambler, and the compulsive eater all feel the same way about their respective addictions. They rationalize their actions based on *their present level of awareness*, however faulty it may be.

The major stumbling block to changing our awareness is that we refuse to recognize that our "mistaken certainties" have distorted our perception. This is why it is important, from time to time, to challenge our beliefs to see if we may be operating from the wrong viewpoint.

The beliefs of a person who has a normal, wholesome personality undergo a constant process of reorganization, but the neurotic personality clings to his beliefs, false and distorted though they may be. Usually the only way the neurotic will change is when a major crisis forces him to alter his old self-defeating habit patterns.

If your mind has been programmed or conditioned to accept false and distorted concepts and values, you will develop a lifestyle to justify them. You will assume that something is true, even though it is false. Then, seeking to prove you are right, you will collect the facts and make them fit. You become like a dog chasing its tail. One false belief leads to another until you can no longer function rationally.

YOUR NUMBER ONE PRIORITY

Your number one priority in life is the *expansion of your awareness*. By expanding your awareness, you will remove the "mistaken certainties" that have been keeping you from being the self-confident person you would like to be. You do this by:

1. Ceasing to automatically and arbitrarily defend your personal viewpoints of "right" and "wrong." Defending them keeps you in ignorance by blocking the reception of new ideas.

2. Reassessing your concepts, values, beliefs, ideals, assumptions, defenses, aggressions, goals, hopes, and compulsions.

3. Reorganizing and understanding your real *needs* and *motivations*.

4. Learning to trust your intuition.

5. Observing your mistakes and trying to correct them; being aware that herein lie some of the most valuable lessons you'll ever learn.

6. Loving yourself and others.

7. Learning to listen without prejudging and automatically thinking, "This is good; that is bad." Training yourself to listen to WHAT is being said without the necessity of believing it.

8. Noticing what you are defending most of the time.

9. Realizing that your new awareness will provide you with the means and motivation to change for the better.

Begin to ask yourself, "Are my beliefs *rational*? Could I be mistaken?" If another person held your beliefs, you would be able to be very objective. You would, no doubt, present a convincing case why they may be wrong. Learn to view your own beliefs in this manner. Question EVERYTHING and draw your own conclusion only after you have considered all the possibilities.

There is a positive answer only when the individual is willing to fulfill the demands of rigorous
self-examination and self-knowledge. If he follows
through his intention, he will not only discover
some important truth about himself, but will have
gained a psychological advantage. He will set his
hand, as it were, to a declaration of his own human
dignity and take the first step towards the foundation of his consciousness.

—CARL JUNG

WHY YOU CAN CHANGE

The starting point of all change is when we change our DOM-
INANT BELIEFS that have been limiting our awareness. It is
possible to do this because *we make our own world.*

Change is affected through our subconscious mind and
imagination. As Professor James pointed out, it begins with
changing *the inner aspects of our thinking.* We know from
experience that an *outward* change will come *after* we change
from *within.*

By changing our DOMINANT THOUGHTS OR BE-
LIEFS, we change our inner awareness and hence our outer
circumstances.

In the familiar story of *Alice in Wonderland*, Alice had a
problem. Before she could understand her new world, she had
to accept *new truths* about old, familiar things. She had to make
adjustments to her new world. If you remember the story, she
met some playing cards. She observed that the playing cards
had two sides. If she wanted to really know the whole person,

she had to see both sides of the cards. In other words, she had to get the TOTAL PICTURE. This is the way it must be with our life.

Before we can change our life to a more positive experience, we must challenge anything that is not working in our lives. This allows us to start building that bridge between where we are now and where we would like to be, and from what we are now to what we would like to become.

> The first reason for man's inner slavery is his ignorance, and above all, his ignorance of himself. Without self-knowledge, without understanding the workings and function of his machine, man cannot be free, he cannot govern himself, and he will always remain a slave, the plaything of forces acting upon him. This is why in all ancient teachings the first demand at the beginning of the way to liberation was to "Know Thyself."
>
> —G. I. GURDJIEFF

Up to now, your greatest problem has been ignorance of *who you are* and *who you were meant to be*. The wrong self-image has kept you from releasing your unlimited potential. You are like a bird in a cage, which has no idea of how much space exists outside. Your "mistaken certainties" have prevented you from realizing how truly worthy, capable, and unique you are.

Bondage or Liberty?

A self-confident personality is not possible until we build a solid foundation of self-reliance. Many people think that a person who is self-reliant must be aloof, disinterested, or unfriendly toward others. This is a total misconception. By not being dependent, the self-reliant person can relate to others with compassion and empathy while, at the same time, retaining self-confidence and poise. Able to stand on his or her own two feet, he or she does not feel the need to manipulate others.

The main deterrent to self-reliance is the mistaken certainty that others are smarter, wiser, or more intelligent than we are. This causes us to look to others for our happiness and welfare. The person who is dependent in this sense must always reach out to something external. He wants people, circumstances, conditions, or God to do for him what he should be doing for himself. This causes him to depend, manipulate, conform, compare, and compete.

In this chapter, we shall learn how these destructive habits

act as deterrents to building a self-confident personality. But
first, a word about self-reliance.

SELF-RELIANCE

Self-reliance is not only the belief that you can handle things
and become successful; it is something more than that. It
is having the courage to listen to your inner promptings for
a hint of the kind of success you truly desire. It means taking
your cue from *yourself*—not listening to something or someone
outside yourself to get an idea of what you should be, do, or
have. When we learn to read the "signs" correctly and follow
our intuition, we can begin to trust ourselves and not follow the
beat of someone else's drum.

RECOGNIZING AND BREAKING
THE DEPENDENCY HABIT

Dependency is slavery by mutual agreement. It is degrading
for both the person who is dependent and the person who
is being depended upon. Both parties are equally lacking in self-
reliance, for such a relationship flourishes on mutual exploita-
tion.

The most unfortunate aspect of dependency is that when you
think you are dependent on another individual—you are! You
neglect to develop the necessary self-reliance to meet and solve
your own problems.

A sure sign of dependency is when you habitually *look up*
to others as superior. The moment you begin to compare your-

self with *anyone* you are subjecting yourself to *psychological slavery.*

The habit of leaning and depending is so ingrained in certain individuals that they abdicate all personal authority in favor of another person, philosophy, or religion. They feel that they will be secure if they can find a person, organization, or religion that they can cling to with blind devotion. They allow this person, organization, or religion to be responsible for their happiness. And, of course, this includes the luxury of having someone or something to blame whenever failure occurs.

The leaning, dependent individual is at the mercy of those around him. Believing others smarter than himself, he is always looking for someone to lean on when a new problem confronts him. Subordinate to those upon whom he depends, their advice becomes a *command* that he feels compelled to follow. And often there is more than one "advisor," so he is in a constant state of exhaustion as he tries to decide whose advice to follow.

Advice is everywhere. Most of it is free and not worth the price. You usually have a dozen or more "unpaid advisors" who are more than happy to give you their opinion. But since others are generally engrossed in their own problems and do not know what you really "should," "ought," or "must" do, you invariably get the wrong advice.

Indeed, accepting advice from someone who is not qualified to dispense it is like going to a plumber to get your teeth fixed. Most people can't solve their own problems, so how can they advise you to do what they haven't been able to accomplish themselves?

Overcoming dependency isn't easy. We have been conditioned since childhood to look to others for our welfare, guidance, and wisdom. But while dependency plays a role in our upbringing and education, it was never intended to obliterate individual identity. Each one of us is born with the innate ability to resolve whatever difficulties we face.

Read this and mark it well. NO ONE CAN EVER LET YOU DOWN IF YOU ARE NOT LEANING ON THEM. No one can hurt your feelings, make you unhappy, lonely, angry, or disappointed if you are not dependent on them for your welfare, inspiration, love, or motivation.

The person who is self-reliant does not need to find a master to lean on. He is able to meet life's challenges with confidence and power by looking at each situation in the light of *reality*. He sees things as they *are*, not as he would like them to be; and he refuses to let his life be dominated by resisting reality.

Once you have developed self-reliance, you do not have to procrastinate, escape, or evade what is facing you because you have the confidence to meet each life situation with self-assurance and poise. You are free from worry because you know that you are in full control. You are not separated from your source of Power. You do not need repeated doses of inspiration and stimulation from others to do what you have to do. Instead, you go through life with the realization that the internal Power within you is greater than any problem that faces you.

OVERCOMING THE NEED TO MANIPULATE

As a child, you neither knew nor cared about what was going on in the world around you. Your only concern was your own welfare. Helplessness made you dependent on what others would give you and do for you. Your greatest happiness was being fed, held, and fondled. Your main concern was to get as much attention as possible.

You quickly discovered that, if you started to cry, you could summon an adult to take care of your needs. Even if you just got bored, you could start crying and someone would usually appear to comfort you. Smiling, too, worked exceptionally well. So you soon learned to smile when you were picked up and cry when you were put down.

This simple exercise in manipulation set the pace for the rest of your life. Your entire childhood was spent developing skills that would make a good impression on others and influence them to pay attention to you. Thus, even at this early point in your life, you were programming yourself to depend on other people's approval, and to feel rejected when others disapproved. As a child, behavior like this was excusable, but as an adult, it is self-defeating. If you are still trying to manipulate others *to do that which you are sufficiently capable of doing yourself*, you cannot consider yourself emotionally mature.

A growing habit in our culture is to do more and more for children and expect less and less. Parents guilty of this are unwittingly cheating their offspring by allowing them to be dependent for things they should be doing for themselves. By spending their first eighteen years leaning and depending on others, children are cast in the role of prisoners with good behavior privileges. It is interesting to note that this is a human phenomenon. Shortly after birth, all other species of animal push their young out into the world where they soon learn independence.

The greatest gift any parent can give their children is to help them to become self-confident by making them self-reliant. Children should be given as much responsibility as they can handle at any age level. Only through independence will they learn the joy and privilege and human dignity of standing on their own two feet.

It is a basic responsibility of parents to assist children in making a smooth transition from dependency to self-reliance. Children should be allowed to make and learn from their mistakes. If not, it is a small wonder that, later in life, when they must do something on their own, they say, "I can't do it!" Unless they are sure of the outcome, they refuse to attempt anything because overprotective parents have always cushioned the way.

Every time you do something that someone is sufficiently capable of doing for himself, you are literally stealing from that person. The more you care for someone, the more alert you must be to see that you are not depriving them of the opportunity to *think* and *do* for themselves, whatever the physical or emotional consequences. This is true not only in parent-child relationships, but in marriage, family, and all interpersonal relationships as well. We cannot live other people's lives or bear their burdens, no matter how much we love them.

The umbilical cord should be cut when children reach their early teens. I believe that they should be required to find *their own living quarters* no later than the age of eighteen or upon completing school. Many parents will rebel against this idea with what, to them, seem to be logical reasons. But the fact still remains that nothing builds more self-reliance in a young adult than having to live alone.

It is interesting that almost without exception, the people who have achieved outstanding success in all fields of endeavor, including business, government, arts, and sciences, are people who either were separated from their parents through hardship, or who decided to emancipate themselves in their young adult years.

We hear such excuses as, "We want to help them through school." "It will help them financially to live at home." "It's just until they get going." "They can't possibly afford their own place *and* go to school" and so on. On the surface it may seem like the parent is doing this for the child, but usually the motivation is *satisfying his or her own needs.*

Parents who accept and cultivate this attitude only delay and make more difficult the ultimate day of decision when their children must face the adult world on their own. Through the mistaken use of parental love, they have encouraged their offspring to continue to lean, depend and expect to receive help and support from others as if they were still small children.

Now, let's get our perspective here. We are not saying that you should not help or give to your child, mate, or family. What we are saying is that you must allow them the individual freedom *to do what they feel they must do in order to grow and develop.* Assisting them is where the giving comes in. Give them love, encouragement and recognition for their accomplishments. These are the vital elements of growth that they cannot supply for *themselves.* Even financial assistance should be considered carefully. There is nothing wrong with wanting to help the child financially, but financial assistance should be offered with a provision for its ultimate repayment.

Individuals who have not developed self-reliance have no alternative but to use manipulation to get what they want. If you are not self-reliant, you have to depend on your skill at influencing people to serve you and fulfill your needs. *If you do use others as a vehicle to get through life, you cannot possibly go faster or further than you can convince them to take you.* If you are a parent, always be aware of any actions that will cause your child to remain in bondage, because he or she will pay dearly later in life.

THE FATAL DECISION OF CONFORMITY

Most of us grew up never having to make any major decisions. Adults frequently deprived us of this responsibility and made them for us. If we tried to make a decision or state an opinion, it was never given any importance. Our parents were the final authority. We either agreed to their demands or else tried to talk our way out of what they wanted us to do.

As we entered adolescence, it became apparent that we would soon have to decide what was best for us. This can be a frightening experience, as the average teenager goes forth into the adult world with very little preparation for what lies ahead. Our home training and system of education have largely ignored this vital and necessary part of our growth.

It is at this stage of our lives that we make the fatal decision to conform. As children, we were trained to obey or suffer the consequences so it is little wonder that, as we enter adulthood, most of us choose to perpetuate conformity as the easiest and most expedient approach to life. We prefer not to rock the boat because our need for approval is usually far stronger than our desire to do what we really want.

Conformity is one of the greatest psychological evils of humankind. The person caught in this destructive habit rarely reaches his or her goals. He wants to be a great person, be independent, and do important things. But he can't. His primary motivation to always seek approval prevents him.

The conformist is filled with the need for approval. He can never get *enough*. He runs from one person to another seeking compliments and endorsements for his behavior and actions. As a child, he turned to parents and teachers; when he started to work, he turned to his boss and fellow workers; in marriage, he turns to his mate. He must always have someone around to pat him on the head and tell him he is doing a good job. This bolsters his poor self-esteem. By constantly seeking approval, he escapes from the responsibility of creating his own success and happiness and becomes totally dependent on others for his well being. Indeed, he is their psychological slave—a person who can no longer imagine what life would be like if he approached it in a self-reliant manner.

Remember what we said earlier? The opposite of bravery is not cowardice but conformity. We should never invest another human being with the power to either build or wreck our lives, or dominate our initiative.

HOW COMPARISON BREEDS FEAR

Comparison is a sign of poor self-esteem. The person who compares himself to others lives in a state of fear. He fears those he imagines are above him. Believing them to be superior, he feels he can never achieve their level of competence. He fears those he imagines are below him because they seem to be catching up. If he works in a large company, he is always looking around him to see who is looming as a threat. As he rises to greater heights, the greater is his fear of falling.

The only way to get through life, he concludes, is to beat people at their own game. But, as his primary concern becomes being "one up" on the next person on his imaginary ladder, life loses it enjoyment.

COMPETITION—KILLER OF CREATIVITY

All forms of competition are hostile. They may seem friendly on the surface, but the prime motivation is to be or do *"better than"* the next person. However, you were placed on this earth to *create*, not to compete, so if competition is used as your basic motivation to do anything, it will literally conspire against you and defeat you every time. What we're saying is that the purpose of life is to BE, not to compete. As one teacher puts it, "I am *for* me, not *against* anyone!"

Although it may appear that the world is a competitive place, it is only competitive to those who feel the need to compete. Most people will reject this idea because of their childhood training where competition was highly promoted and endorsed. If you ask them if they think competition is healthy, they will reply, with great enthusiasm, that it is not only healthy, but it is necessary! They feel that it gives life meaning, purpose, and direction; that a person needs a reward for doing a "good job." It never occurs to them that the reward is in the *doing* and not in the end result.

We compete with others only when we are unsure of ourselves and of our abilities. *Competition is merely imitation.* It originates in early childhood from our need to copy others. The competitive person feels that others are better than he is and sets out to prove otherwise. He struggles to surpass those he feels are superior. In effect, he is always comparing himself to people around him. The competitive person always needs someone else to validate how well he is doing.

The self-reliant individual, on the other hand, does not feel the need to compete. He does not need to look and see what others are doing or be "better than" the next person. Recognizing his capabilities for what they are, he strives for *excellence in his own life*. The only competition is with himself to achieve greater personal growth and excellence in what he desires to accomplish.

PRAISE VS. RECOGNITION

Praise

Oh, how we love the sweet music of praise! Most people will go to almost any lengths to hear it. They will part with their money, work long hours, and take physical or mental abuse, all for one word of approval. Just like the junkie who needs a "fix," they will go to any extreme to get "high." As they run from one "pusher" of praise to another, they become trapped in an addiction of approval. The more they are addicted, the more they abdicate their lives to others for direction.

Praise-seeking implies that you must constantly prove your worth. Every time you make a mistake or do something you feel does not meet someone else's standards, you feel "less than" others. You then blame yourself and feel guilty for not doing what you think you "should." You keep asking yourself, "Have I done well enough?" But the person who goes through life trying to do "well enough" develops the compulsive need to be or do "better than" others, and so one mistake is piled on top of another. No matter how hard you try to be better than someone in any given area, you will feel inadequate because there are always those who, in your eyes, have surpassed you. They will have more money, larger homes, greater prestige, better physical attributes, etc. It is a game you can never win.

What is it about praise that makes us act like flies around a sugar bowl? It is the replay of our childhood dependency when so much of our existence depended upon parental approval. Praise and blame were the means of control. If we were obedient and submissive, we were rewarded. If we resisted, we were punished.

So deeply is the system of reward and punishment embedded in our subconscious minds and central nervous systems that we automatically respond to any form of praise or of blame. Just as we spent a large portion of our childhood and adolescence in trying to please our parents, so, as adults, will we spend much of the remainder of our lives trying to please others.

The most destructive power of praise lies in its ability to make you identify with your actions. Praise says, in effect, that you are "good" because of your "good" acts and "bad" if you make a mistake or act "badly." Any time you do not meet the standards of the person praising you, you believe you have let them down and experience feelings of guilt. As a result, those who praise you can set you up so that they are in a position to control much of your life. As long as you serve their purposes they will fulfill your needs, but when they want more from you than you are willing or able to give, they withhold the praise you seek and motivate you through guilt. They know that if they can make you feel guilty, you will do almost anything to regain their approval.

If you are to be totally free and self-confident, you must cease being caught in the trap of praise-seeking. Breaking this destructive habit requires that you *stop placing others above yourself.*

Never look up to anyone for any reason. If you stop looking up to others you will never have to seek their approval and will no longer be seduced by praise or intimidated by blame.

Recognition

There is a world of difference between praise and recognition. Recognition, as we shall use it here, is a factual observation. It is neither a compliment, nor a value judgment. It is simply what the name implies, recognition that a person has done the best she or he can based on her or his present level of awareness.

The major difference between praise and recognition is that praise is a value judgment. If you tell someone that he is a "great person" for doing something for you, you are also saying that he is "not such a great person" if he doesn't fulfill your desires. For example, if your child brings you flowers, you shouldn't say, "You are a good boy for bringing me flowers." If you do, you are implying that, if he doesn't bring them, he is a bad boy. Instead say, "Thank you for the flowers, I appreciate them very much." This way you are giving the child recognition for his *action* without placing any value judgment on him as a *person*.

Adults, young people, and especially children, respond more positively to recognition than they do to the sweet talk of praise. They need to know that they occupy a special place in the lives of those around them. They want to be treated as persons, not non-persons; to be accepted for what they are, not what someone thinks they should be. If they are given recognition for what they do based on their capabilities, they will sense that they are being acknowledged as individuals and not evaluated on the basis of their actions. They will feel that they are unique and worthy regardless of whether or not they measure up to other people's standards.

The difference between praise and recognition may be subtle, but it is highly important in developing total self-confidence. If people are not given the recognition they need to make them feel accepted as the truly unique individuals they are, they will resort to seeking praise and become its prisoner.

FREEING YOURSELF FROM OTHERS

We have already seen the high price we must pay for dependency and how our whole effort must be concentrated on trying to pry open the clenched grip each one of us has on the other. We are reluctant to lose the approval of family, friends, co-workers, and peer groups by doing what we feel and know we should do. And so we let opportunity after opportunity pass by, afraid to pay the price of emancipation. Yet, *we can break away any time we want*. So, the problem is not with someone else—the problem is with us.

Your fundamental responsibility is your own physical and emotional well-being. By not breaking away, you are contributing to a situation of mutual dependency, which imprisons those upon whom you rely, as well as you. The fact is that, in the long run, they will get over their hurt or disappointment and, most importantly, if you meet your own needs first, they will have new respect for you.

Nothing can stop you from achieving total self-confidence, if you really want to. But until you free yourself from the mistaken certainty that dependency, manipulation, conformity, comparison, and competition are essential to your well-being, you will not be able create the life you desire. Only when you decide that you are going to do everything you possibly can to free yourself on a mental, emotional, physical, and spiritual level, will you be able to be the self-confident person you would like to be. The question remains—bondage or liberty? The choice is up to you.

The Art of
Self-Acceptance

Recognition of your own true worth is another crucial factor in building total self-confidence.

It is a demonstrated fact of life that YOU CAN NEVER BE "BETTER" THAN YOUR OWN SELF-ESTEEM; that is, how you *feel* about yourself in relation to others, based on your sense of self-acceptance. These feelings are basically unconscious and have been programmed into your subconscious since early childhood.

Positive self-esteem is not the *intellectual* acceptance of one's talents or accomplishments. It is *personal* self-acceptance. Developing positive self-esteem is not an ego trip. You are not in love with yourself in an egotistical sense. You simply realize that you are a truly unique and worthy individual; one who does not need to impress others with your achievements or material possessions. In fact, the person who constantly brags and boasts has one of the classic symptoms of *poor* self-esteem.

On the surface, many people appear to have positive or

high self-esteem. But this is not always the case. One the tragedies of our time concerns those leaders, teachers, inventors, artists, and people who have made great contributions to humankind and yet are victims of their own low self-esteem. Some of the most admired people in history have become drug addicts and alcoholics, and have even committed suicide just to escape from a self that they could never quite accept and often grew to hate.

Developing positive self-esteem is not just a matter of making yourself happy; it is the foundation on which you must build your whole life. If you ever hope to be free to create the life you desire, it is a task that you must take seriously. If you don't, you can only expect your low self-esteem to get even worse as you grow older until you end up like a tragic number of people who are unhappy or, worse yet, suicidal.

One of the best ways to build high self-esteem is to know how low self-esteem is developed and how it manifests itself in others. You will then be able to see what you can do to raise your level of self-esteem.

IN THE BEGINNING

There are three major causes of low self-esteem. The first is a series of self-defeating concepts, beliefs, and values that you have accepted from your parents. The second is a unique set of put-downs, received throughout your school years, from false and distorted concepts of teachers and such things as vocational placement analyses and IQ tests. The third stems from negative religious conditioning with its overemphasis on feelings of guilt and unworthiness. While there are many other contributing factors to low self-esteem, these three are the most important. This chapter deals with the first of these.

By far the strongest single contributing factor to our low self-esteem is the low self-esteem of our parents. This is true especially of our mothers, the person with whom we usually spend our most impressionable years. Since most adults labor under false concepts, values, and beliefs, these ideas are passed on to children through attitudes, actions, and reactions like a contagious disease. If our parents feel inadequate and inferior, we, as children, will feel unworthy and, as a result, will be unable to cope with even the simplest problems in home or school. In essence, the "false" assumptions of our parents become the "facts" of our existence. The following will help you see why this happens.

From the time you were born to about the age of five, your brain was developing rapidly. This period of rapid growth is referred to by psychologists as the *imprint period*. During this time, your brain received crucial and permanent impressions, which helped formulate your behavior patterns. You can readily see that if one or both parents were suffering from low self-esteem during this time, how easily this might be absorbed by a child's impressionable mind.

Low self-esteem started when you made your first mistake and were told you were a "bad girl" or a "bad boy." You misinterpreted this and felt that *you* were "bad" when, in reality, only your *actions* were "bad." The truth of the matter is that there is no such thing as a "bad child." The only thing "bad" about any child is the lack of *awareness* as to what produces positive results.

Obviously, there are certain things that a child should not do, things for which reasonable disciplinary action is necessary.

But these things in themselves never make the child "bad." By telling you that you were a "bad girl," or "bad boy," you identified with your actions rather than recognizing that *your actions are but the means through which you choose to fulfill your dominant needs*. If a child is not made to understand this and believes that he is basically bad, he will develop feelings of unworthiness and inferiority, which will be programmed into his subconscious mind. These feelings will subsequently manifest themselves as shame, self-condemnation, remorse, and, worst of all, guilt.

A low or negative self-esteem is further developed through the common habit of belittling by comparison. When parents compare a child with a brother, sister, or, particularly, someone outside the family, the child's sense of inferiority is compounded. In the light of the flaws he has come to accept as part of his own makeup, he compares himself to children of the same age whom he admires. Believing that they are endowed with more strength, ability, popularity, and self-confidence than he has, a devastating sense of inferiority overpowers him. If parents were to temper their criticism with encouraging phrases like, "You're far too nice a boy (girl) to let something like this happen," this kind of negative programming could be largely prevented.

Lack of recognition or appreciation of the child's uniqueness is another parental failing. Most parents pay little regard to their children's feelings, desires, and opinions, rebuffing them with such maxims as, "Children should be seen and not heard!" and "Mother/Father knows best!" Often, they take disagreement as either a personal affront or out-and-out disrespect. Leading child psychologists agree that this attitude is due to the parent's low self-esteem that manifests itself as the need to always be *right*.

It is a disturbing fact that a large number of parents lead their lives vicariously through their children. Having decided that their child should be everything they secretly yearned to be and are not, they push the child beyond his or her capability. They want their own unrealized dreams of accomplishment to become reality through their children. Of course, this is done at the child's expense. What such parents fail to recognize is that the child is unable to meet their unreasonably high standards simply because he or she has not developed—or may not even have—the emotional, mental, or physical capacity to do so.

Physical appearance is also a major cause of low self-esteem, much more than is realized. A number of children suffer from physical, mental, and emotional handicaps because of an unusual or abnormal physical appearance. By constantly bringing this to their attention and telling them that they are "too fat," "too tall," "too slow," etc., they develop deep feelings of inferiority that are difficult to overcome.

Some parents place high value on money and possessions. The child identifies with this and is imprisoned by a materialistic lifestyle, which demands that he struggle and strive for material success. Later in life the child often marries for money and pays a very high price for what he or she gets.

If a high value is placed on money and material possessions, it is not unusual for the child to grow up spending money he doesn't have on things he doesn't need to impress people he doesn't know. As materialism destroys the child's perception of his own true worth, he is committed to a life of chasing wealth to compensate for feelings of inferiority.

The previous chapter explains how most parents completely miss the mark when it comes to developing self-reliance in their offspring. Overpowering, overpermissive, or overpossessive parents are usually the ones who turn their child into an emotional cripple. Deprived of the necessary motivation to face life situations with self-confidence and poise, the child procrastinates and takes the path of least resistance. Lack of self-reliance fosters feelings of inadequacy, which in turn also forms the basis of low self-esteem.

Contrary to common belief, raising a child through a system based primarily on reward and punishment is guaranteed to perpetuate low self-esteem. The child must be permitted, without fear of punishment, to make as many mistakes as necessary to learn his lessons. Once he has learned them, most likely he will never have to repeat them. He will know that, whatever he does, he either earns his own rewards or suffers the consequences of his mistakes. The earlier he realizes this, the better!

The most damaging aspect of low self-esteem is that we pass it from one generation to another. Research has tragically demonstrated that suicides follow along family lines. After what you have just read, this should not surprise you. It is easy to see that if low self-esteem is inherited, in some cases the resulting manifestation will be extreme.

Besides contaminating our children with our low self-esteem, we tend to contaminate everyone with whom we come in contact. If we are in a position to influence others, such as teachers or clergy, we spread the disease to those who look to us for leadership and inspiration. They intuitively sense our lack of self-worth and poor self-esteem and inevitably begin to take on portions of what they identify and associate with us. I have counseled hundreds of individuals who have lacked the necessary self-confidence to meet life situations successfully. Each one of them was the product of the low self-esteem that was passed on to them from home, school, and/or negative religious conditioning.

Low self-esteem has many manifestations or addictions. These can be described as the *means* and *habits* we develop to *escape* the demands of everyday living. They are simply alibis that permit us to temporarily avoid facing up to personal reality. The severity of the addiction we choose is in direct proportion to our sense of inadequacy and fear of having to justify who and what we are. The addicted person uses his alibi to cover up the low self-esteem he doesn't want others to see.

THE MAJOR ADDICTIONS OF A PERSON WITH LOW SELF-ESTEEM

● Blaming and Complaining

We blame others and complain to and about them because we refuse to accept the fact that *we* are responsible for *everything* that happens to us. It is much easier to blame someone else than to say, "It is *I* who has the problem" or "It is *I* who must change." The person who habitually complains and blames others feels inadequate and tries to build himself up by putting other people down.

● Fault Finding

We find fault with others because they do not accept or comply with our own set of values. We compensate for our feelings of inadequacy by trying to make ourselves *right* and make them *wrong*. Notice that we frequently do not like it when they do the things we most dislike about ourselves. When we find fault with their actions, in effect we are saying, "I don't like *myself* for doing that, so I can't let *you* get away with it." It is psychologically true that we tend to dislike most in other people those faults or weaknesses that we have within ourselves.

Need For Attention and Approval

Many people have a compulsive need for attention and approval. They are unable to recognize and appreciate themselves as worthy, adequate individuals of importance. They have a compulsive need for continuous confirmation that they are "OK," and that others accept and approve of them.

Lack of Close Friends

Persons with low self-esteem usually do not have close friends. Because they do not like themselves, they generally choose to be either "loners," living their lives apart from others, or manifest the opposite behavior pattern and become aggressive, overpowering, critical, and demanding. Neither type of personality is conducive to friendship.

Aggressive Need to Win

If we have an obsession with winning or being right all the time, we are suffering from a desperate need to prove ourselves to those around us. We try to do this through our achievements. Our motivation is always to receive acceptance and approval. The whole idea is to be, in some way, "better than" the next person.

Overindulgence

People who "cannot live with themselves" because they do not like the way they are usually try to satisfy their needs through a form of substitution. Feeling deprived and hurt, they seek mental and physical "opiates" to dull the ache. They medicate themselves with food, drugs, alcohol, or tobacco to get temporary sensual satisfaction. This allows them to temporarily cover up their emotional pain and poor self-esteem. Overindulgence compensates for feelings of self-rejection. It gives them a temporary reprieve from facing reality and the growing need to change their habits.

Depression

We get depressed because we think something *outside of ourselves* is keeping us from having what we want. We become totally discouraged with ourselves because we feel out of control, inadequate, and unworthy. The frustration and anxiety in trying to live up to our own expectations and those of others cause us to have low self-esteem.

Greed and Selfishness

Persons who are greedy and selfish have an overwhelming sense of inadequacy. They are absorbed in their own needs and desires, which they must fulfill at any cost to compensate for their lack of self-worth. They seldom have the time or interest to be concerned with others, even with the people who love them.

Indecision and Procrastination

Low self-esteem is frequently accompanied by an abnormal fear of making mistakes. Afraid that he may not do what he "should" or what others *expect* him to do, a person with low self-esteem usually does nothing at all or, at least, delays doing anything for as long as possible. He is reluctant to make a decision because he feels that he is incapable of making the "right" one. So, if he does nothing, he cannot make a mistake.

Another type of person who falls into this category is the perfectionist. He has a similar personality pattern, only he always needs to be "right." Basically insecure, he is intent on being above criticism. In this way, he can feel "better than" those who, according to his criteria, are less perfect.

Putting Up a False Front

Those who put up a false front feel "less than" others around them. To counteract this, they often name-drop, boast, or exhibit such nervous mannerisms as a loud voice or forced laughter, or use material possessions to impress others. They will not let anyone discover how they truly feel about themselves and, in an effort to hide their inferiority, put up false fronts to keep others—so they think—from seeing them as they really are.

Self-Pity

A feeling of self-pity or the "poor me" syndrome results from our inability to take charge of our lives. We have allowed ourselves to be placed at the mercy of people, circumstances, and conditions, and are always being pushed one way and then the other. We permit people to upset, hurt, criticize, and make us angry because we have a leaning, dependent personality and like attention and sympathy. We often use illness as a means of controlling others because we have learned that there is great power in playing up the weakness routine. When we are sick or ill, others will feel sorry for us and give us what we desire.

Suicide

This is the severest form of self-criticism. People who commit suicide are not trying to escape from the world; they are escaping from *themselves*—the self they have rejected and learned to despise. Instead of facing up to the condition, which is at the root of their problem, they feel hurt and resentful and seek "to put an end to it all." Their problem, of course, is low self-esteem.

Now let's turn the illuminating glare of truth's spotlight on another area of your personality and consider the quality and structure of what is termed your AWARENESS.

THE MOST COMMON
EMOTIONAL, PHYSICAL, AND PSYCHOLOGICAL
CHARACTERISTICS OF LOW SELF-ESTEEM

Emotional	Physical	Psychological
Aggressive	Sloppy appearance	Anxious
Timid	Wilted handshake	Vacillating
False laughter	Lackluster eyes	Dislikes, hates, or rejects himself
Boasting	Grossly overweight	
Impatient	Turned-down mouth	Needs to be liked and accepted by everyone
Tries to be "better than" others	Tense and nervous	Unsure
Competitive	Sagging posture	Thinks he is a loser
Arrogant	Weak voice	Riddled with shame, guilt, blame, or remorse
People pleaser	Can't look others in the eye	
Name dropper		Needs approval
Critical		Must be "right" all the time
Rebels against authority		Absorbed in own problems
Perfectionist		Needs to win
Domineering		Compulsive need for money, prestige, or power
Dominates conversation		
Procrastinator		Does what others want him to do
Cannot admit mistakes		Lives vicariously through his children, TV, or hero worship
Compulsive drinker, smoker, talker, hobbyist		

The Problem of Awareness

Because we are using familiar words to describe less familiar ideas, let's see if we can clarify things a bit, particularly where the techniques concern you, personally.

I don't care what you think you are. You may consider yourself exceptionally intelligent, overly stupid, underweight or overweight. You may be an activist or a pacifist, an office worker or an executive, a housewife or a career woman, an outgoing, friendly person or a timid wallflower. You may be an alcoholic, drug addict, liar, exaggerator, cheat, or neurotic. You may be depressed all the time, fearful of everyone and everything. You may hate the weather, dogs, cats, exercise, bumblebees, traffic jams, or spinach. But none of these really describes YOU.

They are only descriptions of the things you DO or the ACTIONS YOU TAKE.

If you *identify* solely with your *actions*, you falsely perceive the truth about yourself. You are judging, limiting, and even rejecting yourself without justification.

Low self-confidence is simply a problem of *Awareness*. Once you are aware of the Truth about yourself, you will be able to understand why you are the way you are and, most importantly, learn to love and accept yourself.

Your *Awareness* can be defined as the *clarity* with which you consciously and unconsciously perceive and understand everything that effects your life. It is the sum total of your life experiences, encompassing conditioning, knowledge, intellect, intuition, instincts, and all that you perceive through your five senses. Your present level of Awareness indicates your moods, attitudes, emotional reactions, prejudices, habits, desires, anxieties, fears, aspirations, and goals. Most important, it indicates your sense of personal worth; in other words, how you feel about yourself.

Awareness also determines your concept of reality. Your mind is like a camera that is constantly taking pictures of the events in your life. You are the one who decides what kinds of scenes you wish to record on film, and these things make up your Awareness. Your camera may record other people's negative characteristics or your own inadequacies, hopelessness, or despair. You may read newspapers, watch TV, or concentrate on other sources of dramatized tragedy, sickness, or poverty, all of which are absorbed or mentally recorded. As you focus and file, focus and file, you eventually accept these things as reality, because you have the pictures to prove it.

The problem is that truth and reality are not necessarily the same. If your mind has accepted false concepts, values, and beliefs about yourself and others, your Awareness will be *distorted*. Although you will be operating from the wrong viewpoint, it will *seem* like the truth and you will take on the personality and behavior patterns to justify it. This all goes back to what we said in Chapter 1.

Every decision you make and every action you take is based on your present level of awareness.

YOU ALWAYS DO YOUR BEST

Does this statement surprise you? Most people are shocked when they first hear it. You have been told for years that you can and should be "better." And while this is basically good advice, if it is to be acted upon, it must be considered in the context of what constitutes your present level of Awareness.

The fact is that you can never do *better* than you are doing at this moment. *You are limited in doing so by your present level of Awareness.* TO *KNOW* BETTER IS NOT SUFFICIENT TO *DO* BETTER. You will only "do better" when your present level of Awareness has changed.

ACCEPTING REALITY

It is imperative for you to recognize that you will be happy and at peace with yourself only to the degree you accept you are doing your best at the moment. Once you do, you will no longer be vulnerable to the adverse opinions of others. Conversely, if you don't like what others are doing because, in your eyes, it is not "right" or "fair," you have no justification for condemning and blaming them or making them feel guilty. The fact is that no one—either you or the other person—can do "better" than his or her "best" at the moment.

You must learn to accept the reality of the moment and realize that no other action is possible at the time.

Reality is the same for everyone. The difference between yours and someone else's is your *perception* of it. No two people have the same awareness. No two people have the same background and experiences and so their way of perceiving life, their values, concepts, beliefs, assumptions, and aspirations will be different.

The *personal reality* of each one of us consists of the mental, emotional, and physical characteristics we cannot change *at this given moment.* Your *personal reality*, then, is the sum total of your present level of awareness: values, beliefs, and concepts—right or wrong—that you embrace right now. As perception is always colored and influenced by awareness, if your awareness is faulty, so is your perception—even if you are sure you are right.

Every decision you make and every action you take is based on your present level of awareness.

Note that practically all your emotional and most of your physical problems are the result of resisting *your own or someone else's reality*, or the reality of a *situation* that, at the moment, you are unable to but desperately want to change. Your *refusal* or *inability* to accept things as they are is at the root of the problem. If you examine most of your disappointments and frustrations, you will clearly see that you are resisting something that cannot immediately be changed.

We resist reality, or "what is," because we are under the false and destructive assumption that we can change it. But things are the way they are *in the present moment* whether we want to accept that fact or not. Only when we can *consciously* recognize a particular phase of reality for what it is *in the present moment* is our resistance to it overcome.

The key to change is to accept other people's behavior without feeling that you have to "set them right." You must allow them the personal freedom to live according to their own individual Awareness, however distorted and faulty it may be. To do this, you must learn to love and accept yourself first. If you are still judging yourself, you will feel compelled to judge others, thereby resisting their reality and present level of Awareness.

You can only be compassionate and understanding of others to the degree that you are compassionate and understanding of yourself.

If you are not conscious that you are resisting reality, there is no way for you to break this destructive habit. You will always feel a need to judge things as "good" or "bad," "right" or "wrong," "fair" or "unfair." You will believe that people and circumstances are conspiring against you because you refuse to face up to WHAT IS. And so you live in a world of wishful thinking where things "should be," but are not a certain way.

It is a demonstrated fact of life that *what happens to you is not nearly as important as the degree of intensity with which you resist the reality of a particular situation or individual.* To put it another way, you can't help the way you *feel* about things, but you *can* help the way you *think* about and *react* to them. You may not like the reality of a situation, but you must accept it for the present moment. In so doing, you will have control over your actions and reactions.

One doesn't have to be a mental giant to see that resistance to reality is the cause of more heartache, headaches, resentment, hostility, and family problems than anything else. You cannot possibly feel hurt emotionally, or get angry, resentful, or bitter toward another, nor can you ever feel "less than" or be "put down" and hurt by others without resisting reality.

THE DESTRUCTIVE POWER OF VALUE-JUDGING

The basic cause of most inharmonious human relationships is the tendency to impose our values on other people. We want them to live by what we have decided is "*right*," "*fair*," "*good*," etc. If they do not conform, we become resentful and angry, not recognizing that their level of Awareness makes them unable to comply.

By now, you must realize that there is nothing we can do to alter other people's values, concepts, or beliefs *if their Awareness is not ready to accept change*. No one is obligated to change just to make the world a better place for *you* to live in. People may disturb or anger you, but the fact that not everyone objects to their own behavior indicates that the problem is not theirs, but yours. You are resisting *their reality* and desiring to see things not as they are, but as you would like them to be. This is the point at which you start value-judging.

Your motivation to cease value-judging should encompass the knowledge that all value judgments of "*good and bad*," "*right and wrong*," "*fair and unfair*" are totally unfounded because *everyone must inevitably do what their present level of Awareness permits them to do—no more, no less.*

Read this again! Let it become part of your Awareness. If you fully comprehend what is being said, you will no longer feel the need to place value judgments on yourself and others.

Simply to avoid value-judging others because you have been told that it is inappropriate is not enough. You must cease value-judging *yourself* first, and then you will cease value-judging others. This will allow you to start loving both yourself and others. When you learn to love and appreciate yourself, you will no longer be self-demanding and self-critical.

As soon as you start loving others *as they are*, others will start loving you *as you are*. They won't have any other choice. Think about it! Who are the people to whom you are most attracted? They are those people whom you consider your close friends; the people who, no matter what they know about you, never pass value judgments.

The secret of loving and being loved is to stop value-judging—forever!

UNDERSTANDING YOUR MOTIVATION

Perhaps *motivation* is one of the most misunderstood words in the English language. Executives often ask me to visit a company to "motivate" their employees. They are surprised when I reply that I cannot. All I can do, hopefully, is to inspire them to *change their Awareness.*

It is important for you to have a clear understanding of what *motivation* is. *Motivation describes your attitude when you would rather do one thing more than another at a particular time.*

EVERYONE IS ALWAYS MOTIVATED. Whether you are actively seeking success in a certain field or are just plain lazy and prefer to sit in a chair, you are motivated. If you didn't want to sit around and do nothing, you would do something else, and that would become your motivation. The fact is that you can't start the slightest activity without first being motivated. What you must recognize is the difference between *positive* and *negative* motivation: The motivation to do something worthwhile and constructive and the motivation to do something that is destructive to your well-being.

In essence, no one can *be* motivated. Everyone is *self-motivated*. Keep this in mind: YOU WILL ALWAYS DO WHAT YOU WOULD RATHER DO THAN NOT DO. This generates your particular motivation.

Every action you take is a response to a personal need or desire that is determined by your present level of Awareness. Normally, your basic motivation is to "feel good"—mentally, physically, emotionally, and spiritually. If your needs in any one of these areas are unfulfilled, they will create a sense of frustration and anxiety and you will do whatever you feel necessary to make yourself comfortable, even if that action is harmful to yourself.

HOW TO MOTIVATE YOURSELF POSITIVELY

If you want to have a more positive life experience, you must be convinced that any change you make *will bring about the gratification of a particular need or desire.*

Positive self-motivation begins with changing your Awareness. To make a constructive change in your life, you must evaluate the potential benefits for any given action. Then *you must convince yourself that the benefits will justify or outweigh the price you have to pay for them.*

Others may inspire or even threaten you to make a change, but it is *YOU* who must motivate yourself by means of "profit and loss" comparison. To some degree, you have been doing this all your life, only now you can make certain that the process will work *for* instead of *against* you.

The criminals, alcoholics, overeaters, or drug addicts have all gone through the same process and, based on their levels of Awareness, decided that addiction is worth whatever price they have to pay for it. Once their Awareness changes—usually under tragic circumstances—they realize that the cost of *escaping* from reality and a self they have come to hate is too high for what they are receiving in return. And so their motivation sets them on a more positive course.

You will find it most helpful to cultivate the use of two familiar but often neglected words: "wise" and "unwise." All *your actions* and the *actions of others* should be viewed as either wise or unwise. Nothing should be judged as "good" or "bad," "fair" or "unfair," "right" or "wrong." These are only moral judgments based on your present Awareness or the collective Awareness of society.

The terms "wise" and "unwise" do not impose value judgments. They allow you to observe your actions or the actions of another and, on the basis of Awareness, decide if they are "wise" or "unwise." At no time is *the person* being judged. It is important to understand that your *actions* may be "bad," but *you* are never "bad." You must extend this same understanding to everyone else in turn.

I hope, by now, that you can see it is impossible to "motivate" people to change by telling them what they "must," "should," or "ought" to do. They can only change through their own *conscious decisions*. You may inspire, frighten, or threaten them, but the motivation generated will only be temporary to fulfill their dominant need which, for that moment, is to get you off their backs. They will not change their habits permanently until they are convinced that the change will be beneficial to *them* in relation to the price they have to pay. More importantly, they will not change until their Awareness has changed.

TAKING RESPONSIBILITY

You have the right and option to choose anything you want to do—*anything at all*. No one else can choose for you. The Creator has given you *free will* to do *anything* you wish within the limits of your intellectual and physical capabilities.

This means you are allowed to make mistakes, fail, lie, cheat, cry, shout; to be lazy, angry, selfish, loyal, aggressive, rejected, or hurt; to overindulge in food, drink, or sex; to take drugs, change your mind, or do anything else you want. The Divine gift of *free will* is always yours. Free will certainly *does not* imply that you must make the "right" choice all the time! Your choice is only as "right" as your present level of Awareness. However, keep in mind that you are responsible for consequences of all your choices.

You have learned that, when you make any decision, it is based on a level of Awareness that is at a *fixed* point for that moment. You can do *one* thing and only *one* thing based on your current Awareness. Thus you are always doing the *best* you can under the present circumstances. You must give yourself the right to make mistakes because it is through mistakes that your Awareness is expanded.

You will never be free until you learn to be true to yourself and accept full responsibility for your own life and the fulfillment of your needs. But, in doing so, you must also accept full responsibility for every thought, word, deed, and decision, for inevitably you will have to pay the price for each. To use an old adage: If you want to dance, you must be prepared to pay the fiddler. You will learn and grow according to the nature and consequences of your actions.

Keep in mind that nothing you do is "right" or "wrong," "good" or "bad." It is only *wise* and *unwise*. Hopefully as you progress from *unwise* to *wise* actions, the importance of this terminology will become increasingly evident.

In regard to wise or unwise decisions, before you take any action, ask yourself the following questions:

Is this a wise or an unwise act?

Will it contribute to my basic needs?

Will it harm me or someone else?

What is the total price I must pay?

Is it in harmony with Laws of the Universe, as I understand them?

Am I willing and able to pay this price and accept the consequences?

By asking these questions, you will put yourself in full, conscious control of your life. They will help you to build a new

Awareness based upon the knowledge that the person to whom you are accountable for all your actions is YOU. The logic of this is quite evident when you consider that it is you who will reap the reward or suffer the consequences.

THE HOLD OF HABIT

Habits make you the person you are. It is impossible to make a major change in your life without destroying the compulsive hold they have upon you. Unless you are happy, healthy, calm, peaceful, self-reliant, and successful in every area of your life, changing self-defeating habits must take priority in your life.

Most of us have no idea how much our lives are built around so-called "bad habits." We have programmed the wrong responses into our subconscious minds and central nervous system. This causes us to respond the way we have conditioned ourselves to feel and act, no matter how negative, false, distorted, or destructive this might be. Consequently, we must go through a period of unlearning or deprogramming in order to change our negative, self-defeating habit patterns.

YOU CANNOT GIVE UP ANYTHING YOU REGARD AS DESIRABLE

No amount of willpower is of any use unless we really want to give up old habits. Most of the time we want to get rid of their *painful effects* but are not willing to give up the habits themselves.

The reason most diets fail after a short time is that the dieter starts feeling *deprived*. He has the desire to lose weight and to look and feel better, but he has no *desire to give up overeating*. The end result is that his mind is constantly filled with thoughts of food. The more he thinks about food, the more conscious he becomes of it until the desire to eat overtakes his willpower.

We should not deceive ourselves that we can change our lives by self-discipline alone, or by hoping that we can force ourselves to make a change. If a person really wants to lose weight, he must be "sold" on the idea of getting rid of the *habit of over-eating* that has been serving as *compensation for tensions and unfulfilled needs*. He will seldom, if ever, stop simply because he thinks he *should*. To do so only generates feelings of guilt, frustration, and anxiety, all of which produce resistance to change.

Before you can change any habit, you must fully *recognize* and *accept* that you have one. *The fact that you can't accept your faults is the reason why you can't overcome them.* Verbally condemning your bad habits and yourself for having them only tightens their hold, thereby defeating all efforts to suppress them. Feeling guilty just makes the hold stronger. Alfred Adler put it this way: "Either do wrong OR feel guilty, but don't do BOTH. It's too much work." This is a great piece of advice!

We must create new, more positive habits by eliminating our negative habits through substitution, by providing worthy, positive thoughts and actions to replace them. If your parents took something away from you as a child, they usually offered you something else in return. This kept your mind off what they had taken from you.

There are some things we will give up readily. This is because we have placed an importance on these things and recognize their destructive effect on our lives. The more importance you place on something, the more willing you are to do something about it.

POSITIVE HABIT CONDITIONING PROGRAM

Use the following program to condition yourself to substitute any negative habit that you find detrimental to your well-being.

Step One

Write down the following:

A. What negative habit do you desire to replace?

B. What positive habit or attitude will you develop to replace it?

C. What actions will you take to replace your negative habit?

D. What is the easiest and most logical way to do this?

Step Two

A. Visualize yourself as already having succeeded in changing your habit. See yourself enjoying the benefits of your new positive habit.

B. Use a positive affirmation to go along with the visualization. (More about affirmations later.)

Step Three

Observe your actions and note every time you fail to do what you promise. Remember, DO NOT condemn or scold yourself. Simply make a non-judgmental observation and allow yourself to make the necessary correction.

Step Four

Keep a record for at least twenty-one days.

After you consciously choose your new positive habit pattern, these four steps will enable you to program it into your subconscious. It will then become an automatic response action.

If you have established negative responses to life situations, your automatic mechanism will cause you to respond the way you have conditioned yourself to FEEL and ACT.

It is advisable to monitor your responses or habit patterns by using the following three-step formula to evaluate and correct them.

1. Remove anything in your life that is *not working* for your good.

2. See what is *working* for you and continue to program that into your subconscious.

3. Add new things you find desirable that are likely to work for you.

Use the above formula for the rest of your life and you will find that you will gain self-confidence and your life will be full of successful experiences.

Remember these important facts about changing your habits:

A. Recognize and accept the fact that you have a negative habit and place no value judgment on yourself.

B. Before starting to change your habit, weigh the potential benefits against the price you will have to pay for overcoming it.

C. Understand that no amount of willpower is of any use unless you really want to give up a habit.

D. You must be convinced that change will bring about the gratification of a particular need or desire.

E. Above all, do not feel guilty, condemn, or blame yourself for your present condition. Up until now, you have only done what your level of Awareness has allowed you to do.

As a new habit becomes stronger we are tempted less and less by the old one. We must always be aware of our thoughts and actions and keep our *dominant thoughts* focused on what we want instead of what we don't want.

I'm Not Guilty,
You're Not Guilty

Guilt is one of the most common forms of stress in our society. The world is full of guilt-ridden people. Unless you are one of those rare individuals who have overcome this destructive emotion, you probably share a variety of unnecessary guilt feelings with the vast majority.

Most of us have been conditioned to feel guilty. Family, friends, society, school, loved ones, and religion have consciously or unconsciously turned us into guilt machines. We have been reminded since childhood of our so-called "bad behavior" and made to feel guilty about things we did or didn't do, or said or didn't say. Since most of us are conditioned to seek approval from others, we cannot handle guilt when it is imposed upon us from an outside source.

Guilt is the master tool of the manipulator. All a person has to do is to make us feel guilty and we feel compelled to get back into their good graces as soon as possible. Most people can be manipulated into doing just about anything if they can be made to feel guilty enough.

Why do we permit this to happen? Simply because guilt has been associated with *caring* and, if you don't care, you are a "bad person." The truth is that guilt has nothing whatsoever to do with caring. Rather, it is a manifestation of neurotic behavior, behavior which, oddly enough, is accepted as "normal" by most people. In other words, to show that you really care, you are expected to feel guilty. If you don't, then you don't really care. This twisted line of reasoning controls the lives of a tragic number of individuals.

It is interesting to note that, in my classes, when I say one must *never* feel guilty, someone invariably raises his hand and asks, "Do you mean that I shouldn't *ever* feel guilty about *anything*?" Of course, what he is trying to say is that he has been so conditioned into feeling guilty that he feels guilty about not feeling guilty!

A LOOK AT MORALITY

A great many actions that are labeled "good" or "bad" by certain individuals, society, or religious groups are nothing more than moral value judgments based on *their* present levels of Awareness, which may be faulty. What is moral and right for you today may not be moral and right for you tomorrow at another time or in another place, for morality varies from place to place and time to time.

Thomas Moore put it very well when he said,

> *I find the doctors and the sages*
> *Have differ'd in all climes and ages*
> *And two in fifty scarce agree*
> *On what is pure morality.*

Laws that are based on morality are not Universal Laws, for Universal Laws are immutable. They are few, simple and enforceable everywhere, always, automatically, without interference or moral value judgment by any group, religion, or individual. There is no Universal Law to support guilt. Remember, GUILT IS A *LEARNED* EMOTIONAL RESPONSE.

THE SEVEN MAJOR FORMS OF GUILT

Parent-Child Guilt

As a child, you were made to feel guilty by the adults around you and by your family in particular. After all, if they felt guilty, it was good enough for them, so it must be enough good for you too! If they didn't like what you did or said, you were told that you were a "bad girl" or a "bad boy." A value judgment was placed on *you* instead of your *actions*. Throughout your growing years, especially the first five years, you were conditioned to respond to "good" and "bad," "right and "wrong." Guilt was enforced through the reward and punishment system. It was at this time that you began to identify with your actions.

Parents unwittingly use guilt as a means of controlling their children. They tell a child that if he doesn't do a certain thing, he will make them unhappy. Their weapons are phrases like, "What will the neighbors think?" "You embarrassed us!" "You disappointed us!" "Where are your manners?" And the list goes on and on. Whenever you failed to please your parents, it was time for them to play the guilt game. As a result, you developed a behavior pattern of pleasing others first to avoid feeling guilty. You said what people wanted you to say and did what they wanted you to do. You were conditioned to believe that, by conforming, you would please others. And so you developed the never-ending need to make a good impression.

Child-Parent Guilt

In a reversal of the parent-child guilt game, children frequently use guilt to manipulate their parents. Most parents want to be viewed as "good" parents and cannot cope with the feeling that their child thinks they don't love them. To coerce them, the child uses statements like, "You really don't love me!" or "So-and-so's parents let him do it." The child also reminds them of the times they did or didn't do things the child intuitively knows will produce guilty feelings.

This behavior was learned by watching adults. The child doesn't know exactly how it works, only that it is most effective in getting what he wants. Since manipulation is the main concern in childhood, it doesn't take long for the child to catch on.

As you have previously learned, guilt is a *learned* emotional response. It is not *natural* behavior in a child. If your child is trying to manipulate you through guilt, you can be sure he picked up the tactics from a good teacher—*YOU!*

Guilt Through Love

"If you loved me . . ." are some of the most guilt-producing words used in a love relationship to manipulate the other partner. When we say, "If you loved me, you would do this," we are really saying, "Feel guilty if you don't do it!" or "If you refuse, you really don't *care* about me."

Since we have been conditioned that we must show that we

care, we are easily manipulated by these guilt phrases And, if these phrases don't work, we can always resort to other tactics such as the silent treatment, refusal of sex, hurt feelings, anger, tears, or tantrums.

Another tactic is to use guilt to punish our partners for behaviors that we feel are inconsistent with our values and beliefs. We bring up past transgressions and remind them of how "wrong" they were and how they disappointed us and let us down. As long as we can keep this guilt game going, we can manipulate them into doing what we want. When they do not live up to our beliefs, expectations, and values, we use guilt to "set them right." These are but a few of the ways we use guilt in a love relationship.

Society-Inspired Guilt

This starts in school when you fail to please your teacher. You are made to feel guilty about your behavior by being told that you could have done better or that you have let your teacher down. Without getting to the root of the problem—the student's faulty Awareness—teacher-inspired guilt makes less work for the teacher and is an effective means of control.

Our prison system is an excellent example of the guilt theory in action. If you go against society's moral code, you are punished by confinement in an institution. During this time, you are supposed to feel guilty for what you have done. The worse the crime, the longer you have to feel guilty. You are then released without the real problem—your faulty Awareness, specifically your poor self-esteem—being corrected. The end result is that most prisoners end up back in prison after committing another crime.

Guilty feelings over social behavior condition you to worry about what others say or think of your actions. This is why etiquette is so strongly adhered to. To most people, it is a life and death matter which side of the plate to place the fork!

We have become so concerned about other people's opinions or being politically correct, that we have to monitor everything we say and do so that we don't offend anyone.

● Sexual Guilt

Most people experience sexual guilt. The root cause of sexual guilt is religion. Religion has decided what forms of sexual expression are "good" or "bad," "natural" or "sinful." These moral value judgments have been passed on from generation to generation like a contagious disease.

If your value system included any form of sexual expression that was considered "morally unacceptable," you were made to feel guilty and shameful. Things like masturbation, premarital sex, pornography, homosexuality, abortion, and the like, were all "bad" and "sinful." The result is that most people have a variety of sexual hang-ups and repressed feelings of guilt.

Conditioned since childhood on the evils of sex, it is impossible for the average person to enjoy certain forms of sexual pleasure without a sense of guilt. This will not change until we learn this valuable and basic lesson: There is no need to feel guilty about any form of sexual expression that is within one's own value system and does not physically harm another person. More importantly, it is neither "right" nor "wrong" *regardless of what other people say or think*. Keep in mind that guilt is nothing more than a value judgment placed upon us by an outside authority figure.

Religious Guilt

Religion has done more than its share to develop and instill deep-seated guilt feelings. Indeed, it may well take credit for the *Original Sin of Guilt*, as guilt is the means by which religion keeps its followers in line.

Through the mistaken interpretation of perfection, many religious denominations instill guilt in those who do not meet *their* moral value judgments based on *their* interpretation of the Scriptures.

They start with the premise that all judgment is based on perfection. Perfection, they say, is "good," and imperfection "bad." This mistaken interpretation of perfection has limited comprehension of the word's true meaning. If you put ten thousand of the same objects under a microscope, you would see that no two are exactly alike.

It is a biological, physiological, psychological, and metaphysical fact that each entity is distinctly different. Each individual is an expression of Creative Intelligence. Perfection, and everything else for that matter, is relative.

Wallace Stevens put it this way:

> Twenty men crossing a bridge
> Into a village,
> Are twenty men crossing twenty bridges,
> Into twenty villages . . .

Some religions, by expecting two people to perceive God, Truth, and the Scriptures in the same way, have doomed their followers to failure.

Paradoxically, to be "perfect," you must have some flaws.

Imperfections are the means by which you learn to grow and by which humankind is spurred on to create. To have no imperfections is to have no need to develop mentally, emotionally, or spiritually. This means we must allow ourselves the freedom to grow mentally, emotionally, and spiritually untainted by guilt.

It is difficult for someone who has been programmed into believing that all sin is "bad" to see value and, yes, even beauty in sin and error. Religion says that sin is "bad," yet few clergymen would deny that we learn from our mistakes. The difference may well be whether or not we learn the particular lesson *they* wish to teach us!

Some of the world's outstanding achievements have come from individuals whose imperfections spurred them on to creative effort. If you read the biography of any great man or woman who has made a significant contribution to humankind, you will see, almost without exception, a person with flaws, many of which society has labeled "sinful." Being aware of this should enable you to put your own guilt into perspective. Guilt is unnecessary and self-destructive. Having the desire to overcome so-called "imperfections, sins, and mistakes" is sufficient.

Self-Imposed Guilt

The most destructive form of guilt is that which is self-imposed. This is guilt we impose on ourselves when we feel that we have broken our own moral code or the moral code of society. It originates when we look at our past behavior and see that we have made an unwise choice or action. We examine what we did—whether it was criticizing others, stealing, cheating, lying, exaggerating, breaking religious rules, or committing any other act we feel is wrong—in the light of *our present value system*. In most cases, the guilt we feel is an attempt to show that we care and are sorry for our actions. Essentially what we are doing is whipping ourselves for what we did and attempting to change history. What we fail to realize is that the past cannot be changed.

There is a world of difference between feeling guilty and *learning from the past*. Going through a self-inflicted guilt sentence is a neurotic trip you must stop if you want to develop total self-confidence. Feeling guilty does not build self-confidence. It will only keep you a prisoner of the past and immobilize you in the present. By harboring guilt, you are *escaping the responsibility of living in the present and moving toward the future*.

GUILT ALWAYS BRINGS PUNISHMENT

Guilt always brings punishment. The punishment may take many forms, including depression, feelings of inadequacy, lack of self-confidence, poor self-esteem, an assortment of physical disorders, and the inability to love ourselves and others. Those who cannot forgive others and hold resentment in their hearts are the same people who have never learned to forgive themselves. They are the guilt-ridden people.

Trying to ignore your mistakes is just as damaging as holding on to the guilt they have caused you. Mistakes should be treated like a speck of dust in the eye. As soon as you identify the problem, don't condemn yourself or feel guilty for having it. Just get rid of it. The sooner you do, the sooner you will be free from the pain it is causing you. Only then will you be able to live a creative life, build self-confidence, and express your unlimited potential.

LEARNING FROM THE PAST

Learning from past behavior is important to developing total self-confidence. But *feeling guilty about what you have done is not learning from the past*. Learning from the past means recognizing mistakes and resolving, to the best of your ability and Awareness, not to repeat them.

Mentally whipping yourself over what you have done or wasting valuable time and energy on feeling guilty, shameful, or unworthy is not part of this lesson. Such negative emotions only prevent you from changing your present life experience because your dominant attention is focused on the past.

Nobody can live in the past and function creatively in the present. Your mind cannot cope with two realities at the same time. Your life reflects whatever occupies your dominant attention. If you are giving your dominant attention to what you have or should have said and done, the present will be one of frustration, anxiety, and confusion. This is too high a price to pay. It is far better to forgive yourself and, with a positive attitude, move on toward the future.

REMEMBER—YOU ALWAYS DO YOUR BEST

You always do your best. Mark it well and don't forget it! Every decision you make and every action you take is based on your level of Awareness *at that moment*. You can never be "better than" your *present level* of Awareness, for it is the clarity with which you perceive any situation. If your Awareness is faulty, you will have a faulty experience, which may cause you to do or say things you will regret later on.

Because your Awareness is always fixed at a certain level, whatever you do or don't do, whatever you say or don't say, is your best, even if your best is faulty or unwise. The simple fact is that *you had only one choice and that was governed by your Awareness at that moment.*

YOU ARE NOT YOUR ACTIONS

Your actions are only the means you use to fulfill your dominant needs. They may be "wise" or "unwise," but this does not classify you as "good" or "bad." At the very source of your Being, you are a spiritually perfect individual who, for the moment, may be acting upon a faulty Awareness.

The Scriptures state clearly that you are made in the "image and likeness of God." If this is true, then you must *already be perfect* but are prevented from this realization by your existing Awareness. The more you accept this truth, the more you will be able to express that perfection. It helps to remember that God doesn't turn out faulty products!

MAKE A GUILT DIARY

Here is a personal experiment you will find interesting and helpful. For the next twenty-one days keep a Guilt Diary. Observe yourself in action for this three-week period. Make notes and record all the details:

1. Every time *you* try to make *someone else* feel guilty.

2. Every time *someone* tries to make *you* feel guilty.

3. Every time *you* try to make *yourself* feel guilty.

By doing this, you will become acutely aware of how much time is spent playing the guilt game. Every time you try to make yourself or someone else feel guilty, stop right then and there and make a correction. This will change your habit patterns and soon you will cease playing the game altogether.

Every time you sense someone is trying to make you feel guilty, then let them know that their game is no longer effective. The victim must let the exploiter know that he or she is no longer vulnerable. At first they won't believe you because they have been using guilt to manipulate you for so long. But once they realize that you no longer need their approval and will not play the guilt game, they will cease using guilt as a means to exploit you.

The Positive Power of Love

Love has inspired books, songs, works of art, great achievements, and even changed the course of history. It is the bond that holds humankind together.

There are many definitions of love, yet each one is inadequate. Love can be found in the dictionary somewhere between "like" and "lust." And maybe that's where it belongs!

To understand what love is, we have to understand what love is not. Love is not hate, violence, ambition, or competition. It is not infatuation. Infatuation focuses only on external traits and is merely a form of conquest that fills a personal need that is invariably followed by disappointment.

For example, a woman marries a man because he is handsome, then says that all he thinks about is his looks. She marries him because he is intelligent, then feels stupid and accuses him of knowing it all. She marries him because he is steady and sensible, then finds him boring and dull. She marries him for his money, then is unhappy because all he thinks about is business. She marries him because his is sexy, then objects when he is sexually attractive to other women. And on and on it goes! These examples are not love, merely infatuation. The same examples can be used for a man as well.

Love is not sex. You can have sex without love, and love without sex. But when sex and love are combined, the result is a beautiful, spiritual experience, one unequaled by any other.

What, then, is love? *Love is the attracting, uniting, harmonizing Force of the Universe.*

Love is the desire to support a person in being all that they can be. It's helping the other person to grow emotionally, mentally, and spiritually. Most of all, love is allowing another person the complete freedom to be himself or herself and accepting that person without trying to change them.

The problem with many relationships is that love is one-sided. In order for a relationship to be balanced, you must give, but also expect to receive. Your needs must be met as well as those of your partner. The compulsion to keep giving without expecting a return, or keep receiving without expecting to give, does not support true love.

To love means to love. Period! It doesn't imply conditions such as "I will love you *if* . . . ," "I will love you as *long as* . . . ," or "I will love you *when* . . ." Love that implies conditions is nothing more than emotional blackmail.

A child's ability to love is usually set by the time he or she is approximately two years old. This is why it is important to build the child's self-esteem during this period. The child must learn that he or she is accepted for *who they are* and that love (or withholding love) is not based on his or her *actions*.

Often, young girls do not learn that they can be loved for

who they are. They feel they need a man to make them feel loved and valuable. They will often marry the first man that comes along who tells them what they want to hear—that they are loved. Sensing her feelings of inferiority, the man will often play on her feeling of inadequacy and try to dominate her. Since she really does not love herself, she will obsessively seek the approval and the love she didn't get as a child. The odds are that she will end up either in the divorce court or with a husband who is an alcoholic; mentally, physically, or emotionally abusive; or perhaps something worse. If self-confidence, self-acceptance, and the acceptance of others had been cultivated early in life, this could have been avoided.

It is important in a relationship to *preserve* love. In order to do this, it is necessary to realize that you are not a couple or twosome or anything else. Despite the abundance of poetic imagery, it is literally impossible to merge two human beings as one. You are simply *separate individuals* who have found a great deal to share together. You came into the world alone, and you will leave this world alone.

It is sheer folly to promise to love another person *forever*. While it is beautiful to hear someone declare that they will love us *forever*, it is an empty promise. Think about it for a moment. You cannot count on your lover loving you forever, no matter what he or she says, for *love is a moment-by-moment experience*. Yesterday's love has been spent, tomorrow's love is not here yet, and today's love must be earned.

The fact is that *love will only continue as long as each person fulfills a need and contributes to the relationship*. And love must continue if a relationship is to be held together. A legal contract won't do it!

In order to preserve love, one partner must not attempt to

change the other. This happens much too often and is a major contributing factor to break-up and divorce.

Love, romance, and excitement are all possible when you permit your partner to express his or her own individuality. When a relationship is not stifled by unreasonable demands and expectations, the partners will grow closer. The more independent you feel, the more you will value your partner. True love depends on true freedom. *Only those who are free can afford to love without reservation.*

Time spent together should be devoted to motives of love and sharing those things you both enjoy. This will eliminate boredom and keep the relationship alive. Vital, in this regard, is the development of a romantic personality. Without romance, a person's life lacks magnetism, so it is important for you to cultivate it. A romantic personality will increase your magnetism and enable you to attract the people, events, and circumstances you desire. We all need romance in our lives and are grateful to those who stimulate and encourage it.

Everyone wants to be loved. Every stranger you meet is crying out inside, "Please love me." Sometimes this is difficult to justify in the light of our actions; sometimes the individuals themselves don't recognize this as the inner hunger they feel.

Most people believe that they are not loved enough. This is because they cannot recapture the love they once knew as children, and so they go through life trying to regain this perfect emotion by searching *outside* of themselves.

Look at your life. You go to the grocery store for food, to classes for education, to the doctor to get well, to a contractor to build your house, to the hair stylist to have your hair done, to the department store to buy your clothes. And so it is with love. You go to others for love. Like a carrot dangled before a horse, there is love, just out of reach.

STOP LOOKING FOR OTHERS TO LOVE YOU!

If you are seeking someone to love you, you will go through life disappointed. Love begins with loving yourself first. Unless you first love yourself, you will not be able to find it in another. Only when you generate love and radiate it forth until it embraces everything and everyone, will love be yours in return.

But remember, you cannot *give* your love to another person. You can only be loving. Being loving means learning to love your mind, thoughts, body, life, and the God-power within you. Learn to love objects like trees, flowers, animals, sunshine, and everything you see, touch, and taste. Have you ever noticed how some people always have trouble with their automobiles? Their vehicles just don't respond to them. Yet another person "talks" to his automobile and it responds trouble-free, trip after trip. It would seem that even inanimate things do sense love. Preposterous? It has been scientifically demonstrated that metal atoms respond differently to different personalities.

Loving is one of our strongest needs. It has been discovered by behavioral scientists that it is not *lack of love* that causes negative personality disorders, but *lack of loving*. One man proved this while running a ranch home for delinquent boys and girls. Upon entering the home, the children were given an animal to feed, care for, and learn to love. For many of them this was the first form of life they could love. The success rate in rehabilitating these children was outstanding, just because he taught them to love.

DOING UNTO OTHERS

The idea that we cannot possibly love another until we have first learned to love ourselves may, on the surface, appear to be a very self-centered philosophy. But it isn't if we realize that we are connected to every other person on the planet. In the same way that our heads are joined to our shoulders, our hands to our arms, our feet to our ankles, each person is an extension of everyone else. An infection in one part of the human body means that the entire body is affected; to hurt another person mentally, physically, or emotionally means that we are hurting ourselves.

For this reason, we cannot say, "To hell with the rest of the world, I'm just going to take care of myself." Instead, we want to make it our desire to elevate the consciousness of humankind for, like a chain, the human race is only as strong as its weakest link.

SOME IMPORTANT ASPECTS OF LOVE AND THEIR RELATIONSHIP TO YOUR INDIVIDUAL PROGRESS

Remain calm and loving regardless of the circumstances. Love is not a placid state but a conquering force. If someone does something to you that may seem unjust or unfair, learn to forgive that person, for forgiveness is part of love. Mentally note that the situation has come into your life as a lesson. The way you meet the experience will determine whether or not you understand the meaning of love. If you do, you will be able to forgive, knowing that everything will work out for the good of all concerned. To pass "love lessons" victoriously is to reach new dimensions of success, prosperity, peace, and fulfillment.

Learn to love everything that happens to you because your experiences give you a chance to grow in the consciousness of love. Say to yourself many times a day, "I am growing in the consciousness of love." As you do, it will enrich your life in marvelous ways.

Many people go through life hating, criticizing, and condemning others for their own lack of love. These are the negative people. They have a talent for putting others down with joking sarcasm and making them feel so inadequate and useless that they either hold back, withdraw, or just plain give up. Negative people withhold love, recognition, and compliments because they must always say what is on their minds, regardless of how destructive it is. They justify their verbal hostility as "constructive criticism," an "honest relationship," or even "objective appraisal." Their greatest talent lies in the ability to find and identify the weaknesses in others instead of their strengths.

A few years ago, I conducted a seminar for couples. One of the projects was for each person to list ten good things about his or her partner. I offered a prize for the first one finished. What was interesting but not surprising about this experiment was that by the time the first one had finished, some had not even written down *one* item. These people were either unwilling or unable to write one positive or complimentary characteristic about the person with whom they were sharing their life.

It is common knowledge that when plants are praised and

spoken to positively, they thrive and grow; but when they are condemned and rejected, they become stunted or even die. If you have this effect on your plants, just think of the effect you have on another human being!

The Positive Power of Love determines how successful you will be in life. In order to be successful, you must be able to get things done. There are three ways of doing this: to do the task yourself, to get someone to help you, or to team up with others and *give* help.

The first method is the most common, but it is also the most limiting because you are restricted to the amount of time and effort you, personally, can expend. If you read the biographies of great achievers, you will notice that they generally become successful by expanding their growth through the efforts of others. In other words, they get things done by either receiving or giving help.

Giving help is one of the little known secrets of success. You get things done by helping others get things done. If you are a supervisor, manager, or boss, by assisting those under you to become successful, you become more successful yourself. If you are a teacher, success comes in direct proportion to your success in helping your students to succeed; it comes by showing them how they can get what *they* want, not what *you* want. Any relationship can grow and prosper when we learn to assist others.

Love is the means by which we help others to be successful. It expresses itself in the ability to make others feel important, alive and capable of self-improvement. By giving others recognition and assurance, and pointing out their positive traits, we can stimulate them to make the best possible use of their unlimited potential. One of the greatest gifts we can give to other people is to open their eyes to their own greatness; to the potential they never realized existed. This is what "loving thy neighbor" is all about.

But helping others in not a one-way street. By offering encouragement and pointing out people's strengths, we are helping ourselves as well. Not only does this satisfy our own need for loving; each positive action generates an even more positive response and increases our total self-confidence.

Emmet Fox put it so well when he said, "Sufficient realization of love will overcome anything. There is no difficulty that love cannot conquer, no disease it will not heal, no door it will not open, no guilt it will not bridge, no wall it will not tear down, no sin it will not redeem. Love will lift you to the highest dimension."

I love everything I do. I love my work. I love teaching. And I love writing this book for you!

Mind—Your Own Business

To this day, relatively little is known about the human mind and its principal tool, the brain. We are finding out that the more we think we know, the more there is to learn.

Like electricity, the mind is a usable force that has existed and will continue to exist for eternity. Its powers stagger the imagination. While science is learning more and more about its tremendous potential every day, we need not wait for a blueprint to make full use of that with which we are naturally endowed.

The longer you wait, the more you study and research elsewhere, the further away you will get from whatever it is you are searching for. You need not look beyond that which is *within* for the self-confidence and power to solve all your problems and make life as you wish it to be.

The Power that created and sustained you did not put you together so that you would have to read a book, take a course, or wait for a scientific breakthrough to experience life to its fullest potential. From the beginning, the answers have been within you. You have always possessed the wisdom, intuition, and mental resources to express life fully and perfectly.

Everywhere people are searching, praying, looking, struggling, and striving for self-confidence, spiritual development, and the material things they desire, unaware that no one or no thing outside themselves can help—their families can't, their friends can't, their bosses can't, the government can't, and even religion can't. The reason for this is simple, so simple that it escapes the majority of humankind. The Master Teacher reminded his followers, "Lo, do not look here, do not look there, the Kingdom of Heaven is *within you.*" Over two thousand years later, most people still haven't gotten the message that they are personally endowed with the ability to choose and the potential power to accomplish anything they desire.

Education, government, and religion have combined to create a subtle atmosphere of dependency that places and keeps the individual in a state of mental bondage. As a result, most people look outside of themselves for help. They want everyone, God especially, to do for them what they should be doing for themselves. They are unaware that all the wisdom, intuition, perfection, love, and ability they need resides within them and these great powers are waiting to be released.

YOU, INCORPORATED

For the purpose of our study, we shall break down the three primary phases of Mind into Conscious, Subconscious, and Superconscious.

Throughout this explanation, you must remember that you

do not have three minds. You have *one* Mind with three phases. It's just like the air. There is not my air and your air. There is only universally present air, and we all use a portion of it. So it is with the Mind. Your mind is that portion of the one Universal Mind that you are using, and it is broken down into three *phases*. The boundaries cannot be clearly defined so the labels tend to be far more precise than the phases they represent.

The business of living a creative life and achieving total self-confidence requires that you get on a first-name basis with the three phases of your mind and understand the primary functions of each. I call this joint venture of all the phases working together YOU, INCORPORATED.

Everything that is happening to us emotionally, mentally, physically, and spiritually is the unfolding of what is happening in our mind, that tremendous electrical power that is able to reproduce accurately all the feelings, thoughts, sensations, sights, sounds, and stimuli from the outside world.

Think about your eyes and how they work in amazing coordination with your brain to enable you to see. You do not really see with your eyes. Your eyes send a message to your brain, and it is the brain that pictures and projects the vibratory pattern of what you "see." The electrical pulsations are forms of energy that have the power to create in the outer world anything you accurately picture in the inner world of your mind. By controlling your mind, you control your life.

As a result of splitting the atom, scientists discovered that a tremendous power is produced when we are able to tap invisible wavelengths of energy in the universe. Mohammad talked about this power when he said, "Split an atom and in its heart you will find a sun." Your mind is really a tremendous, atom-splitting cyclotron. It is able to release a stream of dynamic creative energy that will form whatever you picture and imprint upon its invisible substance and make it an outer reality. An idea held in the mind has the ability to attract to itself all the elements it requires to bring forth whatever you desire.

While sending rockets into the illimitable void of time and space, vast electromagnetic forces have been discovered in the universe. These forces work under the laws of attraction and repulsion, the same laws that control the gravity of the earth, sun, and stars. A similar electromagnetic force exists in your mind with your blood, a principally saline solution, being the greatest conductor of electricity. Just think about the Intelligence that devised the amazing system whereby nerve currents from the brain are transmitted to all parts of the body instantaneously. This same Intelligence works through your mind to produce that which you picture and hold there.

Electricity is magnetic. The world is full of electricity. So is your body. You must build a constant Awareness of this fact and learn to generate your magnetism to attract, not repel, the things you desire in life.

THE LAW OF MENTAL MAGNETISM

The law of Mental Magnetism states that *you will draw to yourself that which you most persistently think about.* And here we must remind ourselves of something we said earlier: No person is what he thinks he is, but what he *thinks*, he *is*!

The Law of Mental Magnetism is similar to nature's law of magnetism. Let me give you an example. If you were to take an iron magnet, it would draw any iron substance to it. But it would attract *only* iron and reject all other materials. LIKE AT-

TRACTS LIKE. Why is a magnet a magnet? Simply because all the molecules are pointed in the same direction. Their pulling power is *fused* together. Ordinary metal molecules are pushing and pulling against each other. Implicit in this phenomenon is the value of unity of purpose.

Whatever you give *dominant thought* to, whether it be sickness or health, success or failure, abundance or lack, love or hate, the object of your attention will be attracted to you. Your brain cells are sending out magnetic thought waves that can travel to infinity. Each cell is a *want* cell and it combines with others to attract *the sum total of your wants*, whether they are negative or positive.

The important thing is to know exactly *what you want*. If you don't, you will attract only confusion. You may say, "I don't *want* sickness, yet I am sick." But what are you most persistently thinking about? What are you giving your dominant attention to? Sickness!

Ernest Holmes, a noted teacher and metaphysician, was approached by a friend suffering from a severe illness. He asked Holmes to treat his *illness*. Holmes's response was, "Your illness seems to be doing all right for itself. Let's treat you for your *health*!" Remember, LIKE ATTRACTS LIKE. Whatever you focus on, you create more of!

People who are not clear on what they really want consistently attract things that seem inconsistent with their wishes. On the surface everybody wishes for such things as success, friendship, love, happiness, safety, and security, but because they focus on what they don't want, they do not attract the things that they want. One out of ten thousand really understands this amazing fact.

If you ask people to list their most important wants, you will notice something strikingly similar about their lists. The items have one thing in common: *They are all positive*. This is because we only admit, to ourselves and others, those things of a positive nature. No one ever says that he wants to fail or be sick, poor, unhappy, or insecure. Everyone claims just the opposite. But here is an amazing fact: Like the magnet with its opposite attracting and repelling poles, for every *POSITIVE* want, we have a *NEGATIVE* want that we will not admit and which, often, we are not even aware exists. Thus it is imperative to know exactly what we desire, for the Law of Mental Magnetism always attracts our true wants. It does not attract our wishes, whims, or passing fancies.

Most people say they want success, but the truth is that they really don't want it at all. They don't want to do the things that will bring them success. For example, people aren't successful because they have money. They have money because they are successful. Most of us want the *results* of success, but not the responsibility that goes along with it.

With all the knowledge, education, and training available today, it's harder to fail than succeed. But success scares most people and so they fail because, subconsciously, they are afraid of success.

There are those who say they want friendship or love, yet criticism, hate, jealousy, envy, and revenge dominate their attention. There are those who say they want popularity and recognition but, at the same time, make their desire for privacy obvious. There are those who say they want happiness, yet go about being depressed, angry, rejected, resentful, and self-pitying. And the list goes on and on. The simple fact is that you will give your dominant attention to what you really want, and what you give your dominant attention to will be yours through the Law of Mental Magnetism.

The Law of Mental Magnetism also applies to the radiation of your thoughts. If you throw a pebble into a pond, you will see ripples going out in circles. These circles ultimately reach the shore. If you were to take two stones of different sizes and weights and toss them both in at the same time a few feet apart, their ripples would eventually converge. In the ensuing struggle for supremacy, the larger ripples from the larger stone would overcome the smaller ripples from the smaller stone. So it is with your thoughts. The larger the thought, the bigger your thinking, the more easily it will vanquish smaller thoughts. Positive thoughts set up waves that are bigger, more energetic and have stronger vibrations. These more powerful vibrations reach their objective because, like the big stone in the water, they create higher, stronger waves.

Science can now measure thought waves. In tests, subjects are able to think about a certain object and project the thought wave until it is picked up and measured by a photographic apparatus. If the subject, for example, were to concentrate on an object such as a triangle, the apparatus would produce a perfect picture of the triangle.

Other successful experiments involve photographs taken of ordinary drinking water while it is being prayed over and blessed. Preliminary photographs of the water showed very thin vibrations, but as the same water was being blessed, it registered significantly increased radiation, indicating that the power of positive thought can be transferred to an object.

Every time you send out a negative thought, just like turning off the electric light switch, you automatically *lower* the magnetism in your body and mind. Thoughts of sickness, poverty, hate, resentment, lack, and limitation disconnect you from your creative power to magnetize and attract. The more this happens, the more you run down your mental power source until, like an automobile battery that has been drained, it finally dies. Fortunately, you can recharge your battery and become an increasingly magnetic individual by using positive thoughts and words. Remember, positive energy creates; negative energy destroys.

It is time, then, that we begin to learn how our mind operates and how we can use the correct thinking process to magnetize and attract the good things we want in our life experiences. In this chapter, we shall become familiar with the first of the three phases of mind power: the superconscious.

THE SUPERCONSCIOUS PHASE OF MIND POWER

The Creative Mind, or Intelligence, has been called various things by philosophers, psychologists, and mystics throughout the ages. An ancient and interesting example of its use involves Moses, who heard a voice speak to him from a flaming bush. When he willingly responded, he was shown how to lead the Lost Tribes out of the desert to freedom. Asked who had directed him, he replied, "I AM has sent me." Undoubtedly, he was referring to the Creative Intelligence in every human being.

The experience of Moses demonstrates that within each one of us is a power center that *knows the perfect way* for us; a realm of Absolute Ideas that *cannot be wrong*. This Source, which we can contact at will, always gives us the information we need to lead us out of barren places into more productive fields. William James called this Transcendental Power the Superconscious Mind. Emerson referred to it as the Universal

Mind. Whatever you call it, just believe that it *does* exist and, because it always knows the perfect way for you, that you can tap its unlimited potential to receive the creative ideas you need to solve your problems and create the life you desire.

GREAT PEOPLE HAVE USED THIS POWER

You can build total self-confidence by releasing your unlimited potential through the power of your mind. Just as an artist forms a picture in his mind *first*, the law of magnetic attraction can bring you that which you picture in detail. Clara Barton used this power. She pictured helping people in distress and from this emerged the Red Cross. Joan of Arc heard voices guiding her as the Creative Mind led her to victory.

The Bible speaks of this power within that knows all. The Master Teacher referred to it simply when he said, "It is not I, but the *Father within* that does the works." The "Father within" is a metaphor for the Universal Mind or Creative Intelligence.

Most people believe that there is a Higher Power that controls and brings order to the universe. The concept of this Higher Power differs from individual to individual and from group to group, but most will agree that it does exist. If you have gotten that far, then you must ultimately arrive at the conclusion that there is some way in which this Power can communicate with us and we can communicate with it, just as all great teachers and thinkers have done. We make contact through the Superconscious phase of the Mind.

We can do this when we quiet our conscious mind. It is vitally important that we regularly take time from our busy schedules to become still, quiet the conscious mind, and allow the Superconscious to speak and guide us. It does not speak to us in English, French, Italian, or any other language. It speaks to us through *intuition*, which manifests itself as a *feeling* or *desire*. When we receive intuitive feelings from the Superconscious, we are guided to the people, places, or circumstances we need to fulfill our creative purpose.

We can readily see this intuitive power expressing itself in the animal kingdom. Watch a bird build a nest. No one has taught it how to build one. It relies solely on intuitive guidance that shows it how to construct the nest perfectly. In the animal kingdom, we call this *instinct*; in humans, it is called *intuition*. This same guided intuition channeled through our minds will show us how to construct our lives perfectly once we become open and receptive to it.

Remember that the Superconscious phase of mind is the realm of *absolute ideas*. It knows the perfect way so it *can never be wrong*. When we learn to trust it, we will make fewer mistakes because we will be guided by *Infinite Wisdom*. This is the Source of wisdom that has guided all the great minds.

CREATIVE POWER CHANNELED THROUGH DESIRE

Creative Intelligence channels its Creative Power through desire. Our entire world was built on the magnetic thoughts of those who had a desire to create, to move forward, and to lead humankind. *Desire is the seed of fulfillment.*

Creative Intelligence speaks to you through intuition. This Intuition manifests itself as a *desire* to do something creative. Desire works its magic through the power of the sympathetic nervous system. When you want something strongly enough, the desire becomes imprinted upon your subconscious mind. The emotion is then transmitted to the nerves and muscles of your body and you are impelled to achieve it.

The most important thing to remember about desire is that if you have the desire to do *anything* creative, you also have within you the *means of fulfillment*. Creative Intelligence would not have given you the desire if that potential were not possible for you. In other words, whatever desire you have, no matter how far-fetched it may seem, carries with it the ability and mechanics to make it become reality. Every person who has accomplished something worthwhile started out with a desire. To most of these people the realization of this desire seemed remote, but faith in themselves and in the Creative Power enabled them to develop the talents, skills, and abilities to make it come true.

What we are saying here is that whatever you desire right now can become a reality. If you desire wealth, you will be led to the circumstances that will make you a fortune. If you desire friends, you will be led to the right people. If you desire a new job, you will be guided to the right employment. But this must be done through your Creative Imagination.

The Golden Key
of Creative Imagination

All the world's a stage,
And all the men and women merely players . . .
—WILLIAM SHAKESPEARE

In the theater, a "dream" is created that, if conforming to the Aristotelian concept of a dream, the audience accepts as "reality." The limitations we have set upon ourselves are just as unreal as what is happening onstage, for we have chosen to embrace that which is fictitious. But while we must accept the reality of the moment, we are not bound to it forever. We can change the future through the use of our imagination.

The personal limitations we have accepted can be broken any time we wish. By persistently imagining what we really want, we can discard the old script and introduce a completely new story. In other words, we can free ourselves of the limitations that are holding us back.

IMAGINATION CONTROLS THE WORLD

"More important than knowledge is imagination." This statement was made by one of the world's greatest scientists and mathematical geniuses: Albert Einstein.

The power of imagination is one of the greatest forces in the universe. Human progress has developed in direct proportion to the collective imagination. In my travels, I never cease to be amazed at the enormous network of airlines. What great imagination it has taken to put it together. Each phase, from man's first flight to the multidimensional concept of mass air travel, had to be an idea in someone's imagination before it could become reality. Like all visionaries, those who dared to conceive of the idea of air travel had to break through the limited thinking of those who declared their ideas impossible.

Leonardo da Vinci wrote these prophetic words on his sketch of the first flying machine: "Man shall grow wings." His machine did fly a few feet, but Church leaders of the day, labeling it an instrument of the devil, forced him to destroy it. Time proved Da Vinci right. Now men and women truly do have wings!

The most dynamic aspect of imagination is the act of forming mental images of what does not yet exist in the physical world. Another power is creating new ideas and combinations of ideas stimulated by and based upon previous experience. *Creative imagination* takes us a step further than just forming mental images. It causes things to come into existence. When we are creatively imagining something, we are actually causing it to come into being because it has been formed, for the first time, in our minds. Our images contain *creative power*. They are changed through the power of Creative Intelligence.

The actual means by which things come into being in the outer world is a mystery. Yet we know that if we plant a kernel of corn in the earth, it will produce a stalk with several ears of corn on it. We do not know nature's secret for drawing the substance from the soil to make this new creation. The image or picture of the stalk of corn is *locked* within the kernel.

An idea is the seed you plant when you want a certain crop. It will produce *whatever you plant*: corn, wheat, tomatoes, weeds, thistles, or poisonous nightshade. Everything depends upon the *nature of the seed*. Whatever idea you hold in your imagination, whether it is negative or positive, constructive or destructive, it *will bring forth its own kind*. Like attracts like or, to quote the philosophers, "As above, so below."

Creative imagination is a powerful force. The industry of the entire southern United States was changed by one man's creative imagination. One evening as he sat in his home, he watched his cat trying to pull his canary through the bars of its cage. As the bars protected the canary, the cat only succeeded in getting a paw full of feathers. This caused the man to visualize an iron claw pulling cotton from a cotton plant. And so it was that Eli Whitney invented an amazing machine: the cotton gin.

Creative imagination can be used to overcome world problems. We must never think of any situation as hopeless or unsolvable. The belief that we are on the path to self-destruction is simply not true. There have been prophets of doom and gloom since the beginning of recorded history, but they have been wrong every time. When things looked the bleakest, along came individuals with creative imaginations who led us to even greater achievements.

All problems are really *opportunities* in disguise. The Chinese realized this. Their symbol for *crisis* is made up of two other symbols: one for *problem,* and one for *opportunity.* Bearing this in mind, we should carefully examine every so-called crisis in our lives for the hidden opportunity in it.

THE CONSCIOUS PHASE OF MIND POWER

The conscious phase of mind power is the most limiting because its information comes through the five senses: hearing, tasting, smelling, feeling, and seeing. Since our senses can deceive, we often accept false concepts, values, and beliefs that have come through our conscious phase of mind.

The conscious mind is objective. It observes, is rational, and is where our willpower resides. The conscious mind may be likened to a guard at the door, protecting the access route to the subconscious mind. The conscious mind screens all incoming data and allows the subconscious to accept only that which it perceives as the "truth," even if what is perceived is not the "truth" but a *mistaken certainty.*

What we see with our conscious mind often deceives us. When we look at the horizon, the sky and earth seem to meet; a rainbow seems to disappear into the ground and railroad tracks seem to come together in the distance. These distortions are the result of false images and messages from our conscious minds. Sickness, poverty, worry, despair, and hopelessness are also faulty images we have accepted from our conscious mind and chosen to program into our subconscious minds.

To free ourselves from the limitations of our conscious

minds, we must turn within for the source of Truth. Truth can only come from within. To continue to look for it externally is to continue to experience those conditions that have been holding us back. For this reason, we must listen to the intuition from the Superconscious Mind, take that information into our conscious minds, and deliberately program it in our subconscious minds to create the positive experience we desire. To do this, we need to take a look at the Genie within.

WAKING UP YOUR GENIE

In the story of "Aladdin's Lamp," we are told of a genie that carried out any wish Aladdin had. All Aladdin had to do was rub his lamp and the genie would appear. You have a far more powerful genie within you right now, ready to carry out your every command. But if you have not been aware of this, he may have been sleeping for many years. The time has come to wake him up!

Throughout the centuries, successful people have either *intuitively* or *knowingly* become aware that they, too, possessed a power that would serve them just as the genie served Aladdin. They called on this power to help them create great works of art, compose, invent, write, build businesses, etc. Biblical scribes knew about this power when they wrote, *"As you think in your heart, so are you."* Using the "heart" as a synonym for subconscious, what they were really saying was, "As you think in your subconscious, so are you."

Although superbly talented and possessing unlimited ability, your subconscious is a *servant* and, as a servant, must be COMMANDED. It can't command itself. In fact, it is an *automatic impersonal mechanism* that will *faithfully* bring about whatever you most persistently impress upon it. It is a valued, competent, trustworthy partner that will supply you with all the necessary information you need to create the life you desire.

We said earlier that your subconscious responds according to the beliefs and convictions you hold in your conscious phase of mind. Your conscious mind chooses what it believes to be true, and your subconscious mind accepts without question whatever the conscious mind dictates. It is important to remember that your subconscious will accept failure as readily as success, and will provide the means to bring about either one.

At this very moment, your subconscious is working for or against you. Through your conscious mind, it senses and records all your physical, intellectual, mental, and emotional experiences and stores the information for further use. The sum total of these experiences determines your present level of Awareness.

THE CORRECT THINKING PROCESS

As we have said, our conscious minds are greatly influenced by our five senses, so it is easy to see why we get confused when we use the conscious mind alone to bring about the right answers to our problems. The five senses do not report the truth to us most of the time, so we accept, reject, and relate everything based on what may be a *mistaken certainty*.

To look at a situation and evaluate the information based on the conscious mind alone is to look at the *effect* instead of the *cause*. This makes us value-judge both ourselves and others, and evaluate what we see, hear, and feel as if it were, indeed, the Truth. The lives of so many people are plagued with one problem after another because they take actions and make decisions based on what they perceive from their conscious mind.

What we need to do is to train ourselves to look within and ask our Superconscious Mind for inner guidance. As long as we rely on the conscious mind alone, we shall continue to make mistakes and become disappointed and frustrated.

The correct thinking process goes like this:

1. Go to the Superconscious Mind for inner guidance. Remember it cannot be "wrong" because it comes from Higher Intelligence.

2. Use the conscious mind to program this information into the subconscious.

3. Command the subconscious to carry out this information.

FACTS YOU SHOULD KNOW ABOUT YOUR SUBCONSCIOUS MIND

1. Your subconscious is only stable and effective in direct proportion to the quality and clarity of the information supplied to it.

2. Anything you picture vividly with repetition and emotion in your subconscious mind will be brought forth by and become a reality for you.

3. Your subconscious will draw to you what it clearly understands to be your desire.

4. Your subconscious doesn't reason why, but records with high fidelity anything and everything your conscious mind presents to it.

5. Your subconscious will draw to you the circumstances, people, and conditions to fulfill your desire.

6. It will not fulfill your goals or desire automatically. You must ask it and tell it exactly what you want.

7. When you ask it, it will alert your conscious mind to recognize the right opportunities, people, and circumstances needed to fulfill your desire.

HOW TO PROGRAM YOUR GENIE

Your subconscious responds to three things:

I. Verbalizing

There is a tremendous power in words. Words can build or destroy your life. They made you what you are right now. Self-talk is verbalized thinking, so the way you talk to yourself has a profound effect upon your feelings, actions, and accomplishments. What you say to yourself determines practically everything you do. Words can even change blood pressure, heartbeat, and breathing.

The subconscious accepts, without question, the words we use to program it, whether they are positive or negative. Positive statements or affirmations build our life while negative statements or affirmations destroy it. Take a moment right now to think about this. Do you use any of these negative affirmations?

I don't like my job.
I worry a lot.
I'll never have any money.
I can't quit smoking.
I just can't get along with that person.
I don't have as much get-up-and-go as I used to.
I don't have enough time to do what I want.
I don't have any patience.
That's the way I am.
I don't have any special talents.
I need a rest.
I'm not perfect.
I can't lose weight no matter what I do.
I've got too much to do.
I have trouble meeting new people.
I have a poor memory.
I always get a cold.
I don't feel very good.
I can't remember people's names.

Of course, the list could go on and on, but it is long enough to show you how we program ourselves, sometimes without realizing it. The subconscious is then *required* to carry out these negative commands and so we experience sickness, poverty, limitation, and failure.

What you must do is monitor your self-talk and turn such self-defeating statements around. The way to do this is to program your mind with positive affirmations. Repeat them over and over again until your subconscious accepts them as reality.

When you keep saying that you are sick, your subconscious is *required* to make you sick; if you affirm health, it is *required* to make you healthy. Never rehearse a contrary situation by saying to yourself that you feel great, then, the next minute when someone asks how you are, you tell them that you feel "terrible" just to get their sympathy. Switching back and forth only confuses the subconscious. If you do this, you will find that you will not be able to make the positive changes you desire.

II. Feeling and Emotion

Emotion is the carrier of creativity. No creative act is performed without it. The subconscious responds to feeling and emotion more than anything else. Repetition, by itself, is not as effective without emotion. It is important to understand that negative emotions such as fear, anxiety, frustration, jealousy, or hate will work with just as much force as their positive counterparts. This is why they are so destructive.

Speaking aloud or listening to music while using repetition to impress an idea in your subconscious will increase the intensity of the vibrations and help you impress the information more quickly. Psychological studies have shown that subconscious impression can be done up to 85 percent faster through the use of music or voice recordings.

III. Visualization

Imagination or visualization is the picturing power of your mind. Your subconscious responds to pictures and images held on your mental screen. It may be said that your subconscious is the contractor that will build your life. You are the architect, and your imagination is the blueprint.

You are constantly running a mental movie with yourself as the star of the show. These images determine your behavior and the kind of life you lead. You have the power to mentally create a new life for yourself. Whatever you can visualize, you can have. If you can see your desire ALREADY ACCOMPLISHED, it will become a self-fulfilling prophecy. What you are thinking about and picturing in your mind today is a clear indication of what you will be experiencing in the future.

Since this is true, why not visualize yourself having, doing, or being the things you want. Feel yourself enjoying them. See the details—colors, places, and people—as vividly as you can. Hold the pictures clearly in your mind. Most important—you must put *yourself* in the picture.

Get yourself a scrapbook and call it "My Blueprint of Destiny." In it, put colored pictures of the things you want, the places you want to go, or the things you want to do. Look at the pictures every day and let them sink deeply into your subconscious. Soon, you will master the technique of visualization and, in the process, your desire will become reality.

THE SUBCONSCIOUS— A CREATIVE AUTOMATIC MECHANISM

You can train your subconscious to perform any act you consciously choose. When a great pianist plays with ease, you can be sure that he has spent years building habit patterns of perfection in his subconscious. His subconscious mind stores these memories and releases them under automatic control so that he does not have to consciously think which key to depress each time he wants to play a different note.

Your subconscious is an automatic creative mechanism that can solve your problems and change your life much faster than your conscious mind alone. Further, it is never limited because it can be trained and retrained. Just as long as you keep on picturing what you want, like a submarine torpedo programmed to seek out an objective, it will forget mistakes, change course, correct itself, and bring you right on target, all automatically!

YOU ALREADY HAVE IT

The key to releasing your subconscious power is to get the feeling that it's working. You must, therefore, picture the END RESULT. Feel that you can get what you want. Feel that it is ALREADY YOURS. Feel the enjoyment and the excitement NOW.

As you picture what you want, your limited conscious mind may try to conspire against you through your intellect. It may tell you that what you desire cannot be achieved; that it is impossible. Do not accept this as the truth. Remember, the information from your conscious mind is limited to your five senses. Instead, trust your subconscious inner guidance system.

If you want a new automobile, go to a dealer and get some brochures. Look at the pictures often. Visit the showroom frequently and look at your car. Visualize and imagine yourself driving the car. Take a test drive. START BEHAVING AS IF YOU ALREADY OWN IT. *Act* as though you have just been told it has been shipped and will be delivered soon. Even buy something to go with it!

Give thanks in advance for whatever you are seeking to bring forth. This may seem strange if you do not understand the principle. But by giving thanks in advance, you are acknowledging that what you want is on its way to you. Once you accept this, conditions will commence to change because you will be reaching for a higher dimension of consciousness than that in which you have been operating. You will be in a state of magnetic attraction.

Choosing Your Destination

A successful and happy life requires that we devote ourselves to fulfilling a worthy life plan. If we do not consciously give our life purpose and direction, we will be like a ship without a captain to steer it or a chart to direct its course. This kind of vessel is destined to end up shipwrecked on some desert island or, worse yet, sink to the bottom of the sea.

In life, so many opportunities needlessly pass us by because we do not know where we are going. If we look carefully we will observe that there is an intelligent Force in the universe that is unfolding a Master Plan for creation. You and I are part of that plan. If we look at the stars, animal life, plant life, and the sea, it is easy for us to see that they are all components of a very orderly universe.

Everything has a place and a reason for being. Projecting the macrocosm to the microcosm, it becomes obvious that you have a place where you and you alone fit in an orderly and desirable way.

It may well be that your problems exist primarily because you are not in your right place. There are things you should be doing that you are neglecting or avoiding. You don't fully appreciate the fact that you are a unique individual with a special place to occupy and a purpose to fulfill. Your contribution to life may not seem great but, as part of the Supreme Architect's plan, you are none-the-less, just as important as the most prestigious person you know of.

Everything worthwhile that has happened throughout the ages is part of the unfolding Master Plan. All the world's great achievements, in every field or endeavor, have been made possible because individuals have listened to their Inner Guidance, which manifested a strong desire and inspired them to set out to achieve it. To others, these desires may have seemed impossible. But those who create have both *purpose* and *direction*. They realize that they are not merely corks floating aimlessly on an ocean, but individuals in full control of their destinies.

Psychological studies in personal performance show that individuals who have a plan and goals for their lives are happier and more successful than those who do not.

At this stage of your development, it is important for you to make a plan for your life, one which will utilize all your talents and abilities. You must take the time right now to figure out what you want to do and how far you want to go. Otherwise, like a ship without a captain, your life will end up shipwrecked.

Look at each area of your life and design a plan as to where you want to go, what you want to do, and, most importantly, how you want to BE! If you do this you will know if you are making progress. How can you possibly know if you are succeeding or making progress if you don't establish a goal or a destination? Once you begin doing this, you will discover the pleasure, satisfaction, and value of making detailed plans for the things you want to accomplish.

One of the basic secrets in achieving our objectives is to break our big goals into a number of smaller ones. Nothing is really difficult if it is broken down into parts. As each part—each short-range goal—becomes a reality, the satisfaction derived from its attainment is a spur to the next milepost. Failing to understand this principle, many people resist establishing large goals because the total effort involved in achieving them seems overwhelming.

A single glass of water can form a dense fog. If you break down the water into sixty thousand million drops, it can cover an entire city block, and extend to a height of one hundred feet. The same is true of your efforts. If applied each day, in the end, they will make equally as great an impression.

In the game of goal setting, 100 percent success rate is *not* a requirement. Even if you don't achieve everything you set out to do, you will still be further ahead than if you just did nothing, as is the case with so many people. It is a fact that goals, whether they are realized or not, constructively change people's lives. They direct our mental energies into positive channels. All it takes is to know what you want to have, what you want to achieve, and how you want to BE.

WHAT WILL YOU HAVE?

You can have anything in life if you will be *definite* about what you want. Most of the time, we are far too vague in identifying precisely what we want. Thus, many of our goals die in the realm of wishful thinking. People often say to me, "I don't know what I really want." This is just an excuse for not getting started. To never make a decision is to never make a mistake! A person's fear of rejection or failure and his need for approval holds him prisoner.

Not to decide is to decide, for choice is inevitable. Not to choose success is equivalent to choosing failure. The problem with indecision is that it creates frustration. We know we should be doing something creative but, instead, settle for indecision and feelings of self-doubt and inadequacy.

You will feel a tremendous surge of self-confidence and power if you take the time to choose a worthy goal and make a plan for your life.

After selecting your goal, evaluate it before presenting the plan to your subconscious. Use the screening process below and ask yourself:

1. Do I really want this for myself, or is it something I think I "should" or "ought to" do?

2. Is it right according to my value system?

3. Do I believe it is possible for me?

4. Will I be a better person when I accomplish it?

5. Can I visualize it in all respects?

6. Do I have complete faith that the Creative Intelligence within me will assist me in bringing forth my desire?

If you answered "yes" to all of these questions, then your next step is to make plans. To do this you must:

1. Have a clear statement of your goal. Your subconscious responds when you are specific.

2. Have an exact date to begin your program.

3. Have an exact date by which you want to achieve your goal.

4. Have a *written* plan of action.

5. Have a schedule to periodically review your plans for changes and updates.

6. Carry a brief statement of your goal written on a small card in your pocket or purse. Look at it often each day. If possible, have a picture of your goal on it as well.

7. Concentrate on one specific desire or challenge at a time.

8. Make up a positive affirmation or statement about your goal.

9. Always go to sleep picturing your goal.

GET THE WRITING HABIT

Most people do not bother to write down an exact description of what they want. At one time, in my seminar work, I distributed worksheets to help people do this, yet less than 5 percent ever actually used them. Most intellectually agreed that the idea was a good one, but felt the details involved were too much bother. They said it was not necessary because they could remember what they wanted.

This attitude is one of the major reasons why only 5 percent of the people on this planet achieve their goals. They are the ones who are willing to write down their goals so that they can track their results.

People say, "I don't need to write it down. I can remember it." But can they? Can you? Let me give you an example. How much do you remember of what you read on the first two pages of the previous chapter? Don't worry about it! You can always go back and look at it. After all, it is WRITTEN DOWN in black and white.

But why do all this? It is a psychologically sound principle that *vision* accounts for approximately 87 percent of your total sensory perception. Further, the kinetic energy from the act of writing down your plan impresses your subconscious deeper than if you just thought about it.

Remember when you misbehaved in school and the teacher made you write something a hundred times? The teacher knew that you would tend to remember what you *wrote down*. The subconscious mind catches up with written instructions, incorporating the information in the automatic structure of the brain and central nervous system, already making it a reality.

You will find the following worksheet helpful in mapping out your CREATIVE PLAN OF ACTION.

SET GOALS IN THE SIX MAJOR AREAS OF YOUR LIFE

You need to make plans for each of the six major areas of interest in your life. Start by using the following:

CAREER What do I want to accomplish as far as my work is concerned?

FINANCIALLY Realistically, how much money do I want to consistently earn?

PHYSICALLY What program for health and fitness do I want to develop?

MENTALLY In what areas of my life do I want to study and obtain more knowledge?

FAMILY What relationships do I want to have and maintain with my family and mate?

SPIRITUALLY What do I want spiritually?

These goals can be broken down into long-term and short-term goals. Make a list of your *ultimate, long-range* goals and also the *short-term* goals you are going to act on *right now*.

Direct Action Worksheet

(1) This is my Goal. (Write a brief description. Attach a sketch or picture if possible.)

(2) Why do I want this? How will I benefit?

(3) What actions can I take to reach my goal?

(4) Where can I get competent assistance and guidance?

(5) Date I will begin my plan.

(6) Date of intended completion.

(7) I will revise and review on the following dates:

(8) What should I do first? Second? (Check when started or finished.)

1.   STARTED ◯   FINISHED ◯

2.   STARTED ◯   FINISHED ◯

3.   STARTED ◯   FINISHED ◯

(9) I must keep the following postive mental attitude during this period. (Make a positive statement concerning how you feel you must act while you are working on your goals.)

GIVE YOURSELF A FIVE-YEAR PLAN FOR GROWTH

In addition to completing the Direct Action Worksheet, take a blank piece of paper and write down a five-year plan for growth. Call this *My Blueprint of Destiny*.

On your Blueprint, set down a plan that will involve new mental and spiritual viewpoints, new environments, new work, new friends, higher income, and a better standard of living. Make this an outline of the best life you can possibly imagine for yourself.

Begin to look for related opportunities that will help you to reach your goals and check your plan frequently to see that you are on the right path.

Keep revising your Blueprint for the rest of your life. Consider it an unfinished symphony, one on which you are constantly working but are determined to complete. You will be richly rewarded.

START WHERE YOU ARE

One of the greatest discoveries you will ever make is to learn to live in the present moment. NOW is the only time there is, yet we insist on wasting it by mentally living in a past we cannot change or in a future which we long for or dread. In establishing your goals, you must be careful not to get caught in this trap. All consideration of yesterday must be expunged from your memory. And the future, which is not yet a reality, must not be ransomed. It must be free to use when it becomes the present.

Many people live in the future and neglect what should be done today. While *planning* for the future is vitally necessary, living in it only produces frustration, anxiety, and failure because, by doing so, one is escaping from the present reality.

To live a balanced and creative life, you must get into the habit of doing those things that are before you today. Strive for excellence. If you learn to perform your present task well, no matter how unpleasant it may be, you will have taught yourself a valuable lesson in personal growth. Although people often delude themselves into thinking that they can do a better job at something else, there is a universal principal which states that *you will not be offered greater opportunities in life until you have proven that you are more than capable in handing your present life situation.*

Failure to perform your present actions efficiently and successfully will delay success and may actually set in motion a situation that will cause you to go backward. Do not try to escape from the present for a better future that does not yet exist. *What you have to do* right now *is the most important thing you have to do.*

NOT HOW MUCH BUT HOW WELL

There is a creative process that the universe is unfolding through us that far exceeds our understanding. By learning to grasp the opportunities that are before us each day and handling them to the best of our ability, we are contributing and cooperating with the creative process. All that is required is that we do the best we can each day. It is not a matter of how *much* we do, but how *well* we perform each action. In other words, it is the *quality* of our actions that really matter.

GETTING YOUR PERSPECTIVE

The attainment of goals, as important they are, must not be permitted to overshadow or obscure their real objective: to give our life *purpose* and *direction*. That is why we must be careful not to let them *lock us into the future* and keep us from living in the *now*.

After you have chosen your goals and set up a program of action, you must learn to relax and allow your new Awareness to carry you forward, patiently doing what is necessary, first things first, *with no fear or concern about what is going to happen in the future*. As the spiritually oriented say, "Let go and let God." By so doing, you will be aligning yourself with reality and keeping yourself open to the Inner Guidance from within, which will show you each step of the way.

Inner Guidance is always available. Seek it out and use it. If you don't, your Awareness may not yet have the wisdom to chart a course that is in full alignment with the Creative Plan for your life and you will continue to be disenchanted and disappointed when things do not work out.

When you make plans and set goals, ask for the wisdom to carry them out. Present the ideas you have *consciously* thought out and ask your Superconscious mind to guide you in selecting the right one. You will soon get a feeling about what you should do. Trust your intuition. Remember—intuition cannot be wrong because it comes from Higher Intelligence. Once you receive intuition, *act at once*. Also leave yourself open for changes and new instruction along the way. The first move, however, must be yours. You will not be guided unless you demonstrate that you want guidance.

When seeking inner guidance in creating what you want, it is best not to ask for the specific *thing* you desire. Instead of asking for a new car, money, or a new home, ask for the *wisdom* necessary to bring these things into your life. If your ambition is to be an artist, actress, business executive, or anything else, ask for the *wisdom* to guide you in achieving it. Wisdom will allow you to create *anything* you desire.

You can pray your heart out, but even Creative Intelligence cannot violate its own law of creation. By gaining wisdom, will you know how to cooperate with the law to bring forth your desires?

Go forward a step at a time and remain flexible to change. You may not reach your original goal but, instead, may be guided to *something better*. In either case, you will experience a feeling of excitement and personal fulfillment. Instead of pushing yourself into a situation that will only cause you frustration and misery, your intuition will guide you to your right person, place, or circumstance where you can be supremely happy.

Life can be compared to a train ride. If we want to go somewhere all we have to do is to get on the train and stay there until we arrive at our destination. The train may stop or change tracks, but *if we stay with it*, we will eventually reach our destination. If we keep getting on and off, we may never get there.

To reach your destination, you need do only four things:

1. Decide to get on the train. CHOOSE YOUR GOAL.

2. Choose the best possible route to get where you are going. THE RIGHT PLAN.

3. Pay for your ticket. BE WILLING TO PAY THE PRICE FOR WHAT YOU WANT.

4. Get on the train. GET INTO ACTION.

Your train is waiting right now. It's time to get on board!

YOU ARE WHERE YOU WANT TO BE

Like it or not, at this moment you are *exactly where you want to be*. Perhaps you are unhappy. You may have a job you hate, a marriage that is deteriorating, a love relationship that seems to be going downhill, or a family relationship that is unsatisfactory. Your future may look doubtful, but you, and you alone, have chosen, consciously or unconsciously, to allow yourself to be right where you are. The evidence indicates that YOU WOULD RATHER BE IN YOUR PRESENT SITUATION THAN PAY THE PRICE TO CHANGE.

Your spontaneous rebuttal may include such excuses as, "You don't understand"; "My situation is different"; "I'm trapped where I am"; "I want to straighten my life out, but I can't because . . ." You may be quite sincere in these contentions, but the fact remains that you have permitted your present environment to limit your thinking. By choosing to let a person, circumstance, or condition dictate your happiness, you have given something *outside* yourself the power to control your life. In effect, you have declared that your situation is greater than the power within you to change it. Your subconscious has brought the negative affirmation you have developed and, as a result, is obediently delivering exactly what you asked for.

RESPOND TO LIFE WITH ACTION

"What holds attention determines action."

—WILLIAM JAMES

A weak, timid, indecisive approach to life breeds inertia, failure, and disappointment. Many people fail to act because they are afraid to make a mistake or think that what they conceive can never become reality.

Great inventions and discoveries go unrecognized when those behind them give up in despair, exclaiming, "My idea hasn't a chance!" This attitude is tragic because the world needs what each one of us has to offer.

Back in 1880, a man employed by the U.S. Patent Office handed in a letter of resignation. "Everything has been invented that could possibly be conceived of by man," he wrote, "and I see no future in my job." Don't be like this man! The future is full of unlimited opportunities for those who take *action* and turn their thoughts into realities.

FORTUNE FAVORS THE BOLD

Remember this psychological truth: FORTUNE FAVORS THE BOLD. You must conceive in your mind the world you want to live in, the situations you want to master, and the greatness you want to achieve.

The ideas and concepts of releasing your unlimited potential can only be turned into reality if you take bold action *now*. Wishful thinking will not make your dreams come true. Learn this lesson from history: "He who hesitates is lost." Undoubtedly, you could relate dozens of instances in your own life when you hesitated and lost. But you won't ever have to lose again if you learn to take *bold* action.

If you want to be free and build total self-confidence, your thinking must control your limitations instead of your limitations controlling your thinking. Look at your life for a moment! What do you see? Do you see opportunity, love, happiness, success, and fulfillment? Or have you mentally set up restrictive limitations? If so, the fact that you have declared yourself a prisoner will make you a prisoner. Once you make up your mind to be free and declare that you are "sick and tired of being sick and tired," you will be motivated to make necessary moves toward liberation. The truth is, you will *remain* where you are only as long as you hold yourself prisoner.

The interesting thing about this is that we do not have to be superhuman or extraordinary to break loose from our limitations. There is really no such thing as a "great" person. There are only "ordinary" people who have *decided* to do "great" things. These are people who are motivated by a burning desire to be free in order to express their unlimited potential. Each day they meet their problems head-on, overcoming them *one at a time* until they achieve their deepest desires. Instead of blaming others for their condition, they take action to change their situation.

Apply this to yourself. Your personal freedom and innermost desires are waiting for you, but first you must STAKE YOUR CLAIM!

MAKING FRIENDS WITH FAILURE

Failure is a necessary part of growth yet it produces one of the strongest fears most people have. As a child, it didn't bother you. If you were skating and fell down and bruised yourself, you got up and started to skate again. Did you consider yourself a failure every time you fell down? Of course not!

Everything you learned as a child was learned by trial and error. Sometimes you were successful, and sometimes you weren't. If you weren't, you simply tried again until you got it right. You didn't condemn yourself or withdraw and resolve never to try it again. Failure was accepted as part of the growth process.

Unfortunately, somewhere along your path of development, you picked up the idea that there is something wrong with failing. You became very much concerned about what others would think when failure occurred. Even if you didn't take chances with your life, you felt you must always look good in the eyes of your family, friends, and society.

You may have decided that the best way to avoid failure was to tackle only those things for which success was assured in advance. Since there is very little in life that we can be 100 percent sure of, your activities would necessarily be limited. This attitude probably had its genesis in your teens when you where striving for the acceptance of your peer group. Most teens would rather die than appear stupid or ridiculous, or fail in front of their peer group.

During our teen years we spent a lot of time comparing ourselves to others. As we looked around us it seemed that our peers always had assets we felt we didn't have. Therefore, in order not to expose ourselves to challenge and the possibility of failure, we began to withdraw. Failure was something that was avoided at all costs; approval was our strongest motivation.

As this habit pattern became impressed into our subconscious, our limited thinking made us a prisoner. In order to function, we created a *comfort zone* whereby we avoided unpleasant situations and established a routine that we felt comfortable with. Unfortunately, our comfort zone shuts off all the unlimited possibilities that exist outside it.

If we are to break out of the comfort zone we created, we must make friends with failure. When we decide to give up our need for approval, it won't matter how many mistakes we make as long as we reach our ultimate goal. Thomas Edison conducted 10,000 experiments before inventing the lightbulb. Undeterred, he didn't classify any of these experiments as failures. Instead, he said, he had successfully identified 9,999 ways his invention wouldn't work!

What we are talking about here is *persistence*. This is the dynamic quality that separates the achievers from the nonachievers and often, surprisingly, takes the place of intelligence, knowledge, education, and even experience. Those who are persistent refuse to allow any person, circumstance, or condition to get in their way. An unknown writer put it this way:

> Nothing in the world can take the place of persistence. Talent will not. Nothing is more common than unsuccessful people with talent. Genius will not. Unrewarded genius is almost a proverb. Education will not. The world is full of educated derelicts. Persistence and determination alone are supreme.

THE LAW OF EXPECTANCY

Time and time again, psychological studies have shown that the basic reason for a person's success is that he *expected* to succeed. Athletes who achieve success expect to win. Muhammed Ali was one of the greatest prizefighters of all time. In his usual outgoing way, he affirmed victory by stating, "*When* I win this fight . . ." not "*If* I win this fight." Now, that's total self-confidence!

Aristotle said, "What you expect, that you shall find."

Expectations control your life, so it is imperative that you control your expectations. If you expect the best, you will attract the best. But if you expect the worst to happen, be assured that it will. By permitting your life to be dominated by negative thought patterns, you form the habit of expecting negative results. Studies show that over *90 percent* of the population has negative expectations.

You may find this hard to accept, but the reason you grow old is because you expect to. You have been programmed to begin getting old when you reach a certain age. At that point in time, you subconsciously take on the personality, dress style, and symptoms of old age. Elephants have an instinct that enables them to predict death. When they feel their time has come, they embark on a journey to the "elephants' graveyard." The majority of people I know do about the same thing!

Total self-confidence is built through *positive expectations*. You can build positive expectations by knowing that you have the power within to overcome any obstacle that lies ahead. So many people have a magnetic attraction to the past. They save mementos, clippings, old letters, and trivia. There is nothing wrong with this, but if you want to succeed, your mind must focus on *where you are going*, not on *where you have been*. Instead of saving mementos, clippings, old letters, and trivia from the past, it would be more productive to make a scrapbook with pictures of *where you want to go and what you want to be* in the future.

Look forward to the future with expectations and then act *enthusiastic*. Enthusiasm is a powerful motivating force and one of the great secrets of success. Derived from two Greek words, *en* meaning "in" and *theos* meaning "God," *enthusiasm means God in You*. And it is this God Power within you that will enable you to accomplish anything you desire if you release it through dynamic thinking.

The margin of difference in actual skill, ability, and intelligence between those who achieve and those who fail is really quite small. If two people are evenly matched, the one who is enthusiastic will find the scales tipping in his favor. Even an enthusiastic person with second-rate ability will often succeed where a person of first-rate ability, lacking enthusiasm, will fail.

When Mark Twain was asked the secret of his success, he

replied, "I was born excited." Thomas Edison said, "When a man dies, if he can pass enthusiasm along to his children, he has left them an estate of incalculable value." And Emerson, in his essays, observed, "Every great and commanding moment in the annals of the world is the triumph of somebody's enthusiasm." The respective life experiences of these men bear out their shared philosophy.

When you expect something positive, through the Law of Attraction, just like a magnet, you will attract whatever you expect. Know that your expectations of today will be your life of tomorrow.

THE SECRECY PRINCIPLE

None of your time should be spent in telling others what you are going to accomplish. To do so is another form of approval seeking. By disclosing your goals you will dissipate valuable energy needed to accomplish them, as well as set up opposition from those who wish to control you.

Most people will try to talk you out of your goals. They dislike seeing anyone having more or doing better than they are, and will resort to almost any extreme to put down someone who tries to break away from mediocrity. Don't give them a chance! Many would-be achievers have lost out before they even got started by letting others—particularly family members—talk them out of what they really wanted to do. Unless you are sharing a goal with someone else, it is best to keep it to yourself.

You Deserve a Break Today

The best break you can give yourself is one devoted to meditation, with its unique combination of peace and power. Persons concerned with the betterment of humankind have come to the conclusion, at different times and in different places, that if we are to achieve our maximum mental, physical, and spiritual potential, a system of complete rest, relaxation, and inner communication is essential. Without this, we can only expect to operate at a fraction of our capabilities.

Different techniques have been developed to help us reach our potential. The most common is *meditation*. Meditation is not the invention of any one group or individual. It does not necessarily have anything to do with any religious group or denomination. No initiation is required, no ceremony is necessary, and, contrary to what you may have been led to believe, no one has to teach you how to meditate. While instruction may be helpful, it is not essential.

All the mystery and hocus-pocus surrounding meditation has

kept many people from exploring the possibility of integrating it into their lives. The simple fact is that the art of meditation can be learned by anyone with little or no difficulty. The ability to meditate is inherent in each of us. Once we understand the basic principles, we can meditate by ourselves.

WHAT IS THE PURPOSE OF MEDITATION?

Meditation reestablishes our contact with the Source of Power within us. It cleanses the mind and makes us open and receptive to creative ideas, intuition, and inspiration. It reveals where we have gone wrong and guides us back to the right path again. We become one with everything and everyone because, as we meditate, we tune into the One Mind of the universe. It helps us to achieve our full potential through deep rest of the nervous system, rest which is deeper than ordinary sleep but, throughout which, we *remain alert*. During this time, stress is released and we are fully relaxed and calm. Just as an athlete runs to train his body, in meditation we are tuning and training the mind to function at its maximum potential. This is one of the basic reasons why meditation increases efficiency in everyday life.

WHEN TO MEDITATE

Begin by putting aside a time for meditation at the beginning of each day, preferably before breakfast. This will tune you in to the Life Force and program you for the day. Then set aside a similar period in the evening. It is suggested that this be at least four hours before retiring because you will automatically be rejuvenated. Your nighttime meditation will help you get rid of the negative feelings you have accumulated during the day.

This or a similar schedule should regularly be followed for best results. Meditating once a day is better than meditating twice a day every other day, or every third day. What you are looking for is the *cumulative effect*. Consistency is an important factor in achieving the best results.

One never actually stops meditating. It is an unending process. Once you start meditating properly, you will never be the same again. The whole idea is to make it a permanent part of your life.

WHERE SHOULD ONE MEDITATE?

I assume that you will be doing most of your meditating at home. Find a place where you can be alone, preferably in a room where you can shut off most of the bright light. A quiet spot is essential, one where you can keep out the noise of the world. Noise saps your memory and kills your chances of being able to concentrate and communicate with your higher mind.

It is a good idea to meditate in the same location each day. After a while, you will build up a kind of positive vibration there that will help promote relaxation. You will automatically associate that spot with being quiet and peaceful.

The spine should be straight so that the nervous system is not pinched but able to function at its maximum freedom. A comfortable, padded, straight-backed chair is good for this purpose. It will keep you from hunching over and help distribute your body weight evenly. Try different chairs until you find the one in which you are the most comfortable and unaware of your body.

Do not lie down. To do so will only make you associate meditation with sleep. Eventually you will just doze off and miss out on all the benefits for which meditation is intended.

BEFORE YOU START

The most important thing to remember at the outset is this: DO NOT FIGHT YOUR THOUGHTS. Many people say, "I have trouble meditating because I can't stop thinking." Their problem is *resistance*. The more you resist your thoughts, the more they will get in the way. But once you stop resisting them and let them pass by without giving them your DOMINANT ATTENTION, they will cease to intrude.

The first thing to do is to slow down your mind, body, and senses. You are trying to form a kind of vacuum that can be filled with creative thoughts and vibrations. If you start thinking that the house needs cleaning or the shopping needs to be done, stop immediately and discipline your mind to return to meditation.

Meditation is like changing the direction of a wheel. First, we have to slow down the wheel. After we slow it down, we *stop* it and then start it rolling the other way.

Your subconscious mind will help you in this process. Once it knows what you are trying to achieve, it will create a habit pattern that will enable you to reach this state of consciousness. Just keep on programming the new habit into your subconscious and it will take over automatically without any distracting effort on your part.

This experience is rather like starting a motorboat. If you have

ever done this, you know that the first time you pull the cord the
motor doesn't start. You try again, all of a sudden it catches and
you're off. And so it is with meditation. After you have experienced this feeling a few times, it becomes easier and easier.

MEDITATION IS A THREE-STEP PROCESS

1. Relax and let go.

2. Reach out and listen.

3. Visualize and affirm.

The following method consolidates, in simplified form, all
the latest findings and techniques established by psychology,
religion, Eastern philosophy, and medicine.

Step One

Relax and Let Go

As long as your muscles are tense, they absorb both physical
and mental energy. To get rid of this distracting electrical energy,
stretch out your entire body and make all your muscles loose.
Then sit upright in your chair and close your eyes.

Take a deep breath and exhale, slowly and comfortably. Feel
yourself relax. It is normal to relax when exhaling. Now flex
or tighten your muscles by squeezing them and letting them
go. Start with your arms, hands, and shoulders. Next, do the
muscles in your back and abdominal area. Finally, relax the
muscles in your thighs, calves, and feet. Take another deep
breath and relax.

At this point, some organizations give their students a *mantra*, which is a meaningless phrase whose purpose is to keep the mind from wandering. You don't need a mantra. The only reason a mantra will work is because you believe it will.

The best phrase I have found is LET GO. Just say to yourself, "LET GO." Take another breath and repeat the words until you feel yourself letting go of all your concerns, anxieties, and negative thoughts. Keep repeating these words until you are calm and peaceful and your mind is empty of all conscious thinking. At that point you will be open and receptive.

Step Two

Reach Out and Listen

This is a mind-expanding function. Every great thinker, philosopher, theologian, mystic, or scientist has disagreed with his colleagues on many things, but the one thing on which they all agree is that there is only one Creative Intelligence in the universe. This Intelligence or Mind is the origin of all thought.

Your direct guidance and intuition comes from the Superconscious, through the subconscious. Remember that the subconscious is open at both ends. At one end, there is the inflow of creative ideas from the Superconscious. At the other end is where it receives instructions from your conscious phase of mind. As you have learned, your reasoning or conscious mind tricks you by distorting your perception of reality and, subsequently, your actions. In order to connect to the Creative Intelligence that expresses itself *as you and through you*, you have to quiet your conscious mind. It's as if you owned and controlled a great Power House in which a tremendous electric dynamo waited to serve you. Once you allow this Power to enter your consciousness, your life will be a powerful experience!

It is not necessary to try to understand or figure out how it works. All you have to know is that it exists and will guide you, allowing you to float through any of life's problems or obstacles. Spend a few minutes meditating on the fact that the same Force that sustains the sun, clouds, planets, and sea is *within you*. Know that you are an expression of that Power. Know that it is perfect. Let your mind float in it. Give it a chance to enter and illuminate your consciousness. *Know that you are ONE with that perfect, unlimited Power.*

If you have any need in your life, or a problem to which you are seeking a solution, briefly state it. Note, I said *briefly*. You are dealing with an All-Knowing Intelligence so you really don't need to *tell* it anything. The "telling" is for *your* benefit. After you have done this, RELEASE the thought. Let your mind act like a radarscope and sense its directional influence. Be open and receptive to whatever intuition or guidance you receive.

Learn to take a listening attitude, as if you were expecting to hear something. As I said earlier, sometimes it is difficult to meditate when you are thinking about your need or problem. But in this three-step meditation, you set the details aside until you have prepared yourself, then you release them and listen. Meditation is a time to silence your distracting thoughts and listen from within instead of listening to the chattering or your conscious mind.

With practice, you will suddenly become aware that you are listening. Guidance will come through your *intuition*. When you receive an impelling urge, you will feel a sudden impulse to act: to do something, to contact someone or go somewhere. This is your cue. This is your direction. TRUST IT. ACT ON THIS

GUIDANCE. It can *never be wrong*, for your subconscious is connected to the Source of All-Knowing Intelligence through the Superconscious.

Do not reject certain ideas or impulses because you do not like them or believe them, or because they are not what you think they should be. Beware of your conscious or reasoning mind working against you. Carry out your guidance. When you get suggestions to go somewhere or do something, go where you are told and do what you are impressed to do. Let your subconscious take full charge. If you do, you will encounter people or circumstances that can help you. I have experienced this hundreds of times.

Just *listen to, accept, and do* exactly what your intuition tells you. If you are told to leave something alone, leave it alone. If you are told to change something, change it at once. You cannot alter your life if you don't do something different. Remember, *if you keep doing what you are doing, you will keep getting what you are getting*. Is that good news? If not, then listen to your inner guidance and do something different!

Step Three

Visualize and Affirm

Take a few moments and visualize and affirm whatever it is that *you* want to be, do, or have in *your* life experience. Any words repeated over and over again with conviction in this state of consciousness, especially if they are linked with visualization, will be experienced.

Picture a mental screen before you. You can change your life by seeing yourself acting out those things you want by altering the images in your mind. The secret is to visualize yourself as *already having these things.* If you want health, picture yourself as perfectly healthy. If you want money, see yourself with lots of money, spending and enjoying it. Picture your checkbook with a large balance. If you want your business to expand, picture the increase in customers or clients. In each situation, see yourself smiling and happy.

Visualize your wishes as clearly as possible. Not only see them but also *feel* them. They are already a reality once you can visualize them in the nonphysical. Do you remember Professor James's words? "The greatest discovery of our age is that man, by changing the inner aspects of his thinking, can change the outer aspects of his life."

Reinforce the images with positive affirmations or statements that relate to what you wish to accomplish. You can select from those listed in the last chapter of this book, or make up your own. Keep repeating them silently while visualizing. Remember always: Words have *creative power.*

Finally, mentally *give thanks that it is so.* This will make you consciously aware that your desires are on their way and will create a feeling of expectancy. This is absolutely essential to their realization. Open your eyes and stretch, enjoying the feeling of a desire now assured of completion or attainment.

The more you meditate, the more you will like it. The less you meditate, the more you will find it a bother. The more you do it, the greater will be your rewards.

The Time of Your Life

In the lives of busy people no question is asked more often than, "Where has the time gone?" Time, of course, hasn't gone anywhere, as the question suggests, but merely moves on at its normal rate while we become painfully aware that we are accomplishing much less than we would like to.

Unlike the timekeeper at a sports event, in the game of life, we can't "stop the clock" for an instant replay. And when we protest, "I don't have the time," more often than not, whatever we are doing is not important enough to warrant our taking *time* for it.

Let's admit it. No one person has more time than another. We have the same amount of time in every day as everyone else. We have the same number of minutes in our hours and the same number of hours in our day. And yet we repeat the same old phrases.

In striving for a fuller, more complete and satisfying life, we hear a lot about the stewardship of wealth and possessions. Less is said about the stewardship of talent. And little is said about the stewardship of time.

Unquestionably, time passes quickly. Every moment that goes by is a time in our lives. Since our entire existence is composed of time, it is of the utmost importance that we consider the emotional significance in how we use it. "I'm awfully busy," "I'm in a hurry," and "I just haven't the time" are three large nails in the coffin of happiness. Continually rushing through life precludes the development of a personality of strength and beauty, and robs life of its savor and flavor.

Every morning beyond our bedroom windows there is fresh air, trees, mountains, fields, or parks. But we rarely ever see them. We turn right over and go on sleeping or simply jump out of bed and rush off to work. And when asked why we keep this helter-skelter pace, we insist that we do not have enough time to do the things we want to do.

Time becomes our master. Yet we must learn to master time instead of being mastered by it. We must stop being time's fool. Neither waste it, nor get caught up in the "no time" syndrome. Instead, we must learn to control it and make time for the important things in life. When we snatch the whip of hurry from the hand of time, we regain self-mastery.

IS TIME THE PROBLEM . . . OR ARE YOU?

The relentless ticking of the clock gives the impression that there isn't enough time to do what we want to do. For instance, there are things you've been meaning to do for years: learn a language, visit some place, write a special letter, take a course, finish a book, do ... If only you'd more time! You're soooo busy. But are you ... really?

People take courses in time management and still end up having no time to do the things that are necessary for success. The truth is, if we really want to get something done, we'll find the time to do it. We don't need a time management expert to tell us how. Let me give you some examples.

Presume I'm going to hire you to sell a copy of this book for the retail price on the cover. However, for the next forty-eight hours, I'll give you *one hundred dollars* for each copy you sell. How much *time* are you going to spend on eating, talking on the phone, watching TV, engaging in idle conversation, or just sitting around? Would you talk with anyone who isn't a good prospect for a sale?

Okay, you're in school. For every A you get, I will give you a check for *five thousand dollars*. If you maintain a 4.0 grade point average, I will give you *one hundred thousand dollars*. Do you think you could find the *time* to study?

If these offers were made to you, you wouldn't have to read a book or take a time management course to find the time to do a good sales job or attain high grades, would you? The reason for this is simple. You would have identified an extremely desirable goal and have an almost uncontrollable obsession to achieve it.

There you have it! The secret of finding time to do the things you want is to really *want* to do them, not *wishing* to do them. We all *wish* we could do more, but we actually don't *want* to, so we just keep on wasting time and wishing for more of it.

When we do make a decision to master time, the first step is not tackling the nearest calendar and budgeting our time.

This is the last step. The first step is to clarify *why* we *want* to do something rather than why we *ought* to do it. This is done by developing a real philosophical understanding of the importance, as well as unimportance, of time in our lives. Once we have the motivation to take command, the mechanics of achievement will follow.

Gaining the upper hand of the clock and the calendar in no way implies disregarding time. Only when we know how to deal with it can we be in a position to control it. By working *with* time, we can achieve remarkable results. But easy does it! The first attempt need not involve achieving a major goal. *The secret of winning is beginning.* Once we have time on our side, our simplest efforts will accumulate the strength and confidence needed for any greater effort.

EVERY JOURNEY BEGINS WITH THE FIRST STEP

Do you want more time, but don't know where to begin? Here's a suggestion: Make an effort to rise earlier! This one step can add one or two hours to your productive day and years to your life. Take on something you have been meaning to do and do it in your spare time before breakfast. Would you like to be an expert on some subject? Study every morning for a half hour and you can become an authority on it. That's all it takes. It's so simple; it escapes the majority of people who keep chanting, "Someday I would like to . . . but I never seem to have the time."

Just because you never started the work, play, or study that really interests you is no reason why you can't start right now.

Time doesn't count us out. We only imagine it does. It's never too late to begin. Time is impersonal. It is the same every moment. It imposes no limitations upon us. Our only limitations are self-imposed.

THE "AFTER THEORY"

You can achieve success in anything if you are determined to make the time. For example, instead of doing something every week, why not do it every other week? Instead of going to the same place every Monday evening, why not go every other Monday evening? By saving an evening every other week, you will have made the time to do other, more important things.

Most people live by the "after theory." They have big plans. They are going to do great things . . . *after* the kids grow up, *after* they change jobs, *after* they get a new car, *after* they finish school, *after* they get new drapes, etc. This "after" period never comes, but they keep promising themselves that some day they are going to get what they want. Now, while opportunity may knock more than once, it seldom sits on the doorstep awaiting our pleasure.

Do the things you always wanted *now*. Or make plans *now*. Or program your subconscious *now*. Not tomorrow! You will never have more time than you have today. How you spend the next twenty-four hours determines how you will spend the next twenty-four hours after that. And so on, and so on.

Get the feeling of adventure. On your next day off, take a trip to the park, the mountains, or a nearby seaside resort. Never mind the weather! Get up and get out!

Use your imagination. Think about getting a ticket to someplace, packing your suitcase, slamming the door, and escaping from the dullness of everyday routine. Even if the journey is short, think of the thrill of saying, "I'm going away next week."

Want to travel to foreign countries? The stepping-stone is making time. Plan and get going. Don't wait a moment longer. Once you get the feeling that you are going to make something happen, it will begin to happen. Traveling will become a part of you, and you will have a strong desire to see more and more of the world.

Feeling is the key to expectancy. Get the feeling that this is it, that you are going to break out of your normal routine. Expectancy will set in motion a mighty power within you that will cause your desires to happen. The more excited you become, the faster you will get your wish. By maintaining this state of expectancy, you will draw to you the ways and means for bigger and better adventures.

DON'T LET TIME MANAGE YOU—MANAGE IT!

Frustration and discouragement are always self-created. With a little thought, we find that time, without its whip, is a great encourager. Our job is learning to love time; to value it for the value it brings. As has been observed so wisely, we are taught to save time and waste our lives.

Time has meaning only when it holds experiences that expand life's meaning for us. It seems to drag on or fly by according to what it holds. Once we grasp this, we begin to master the role it plays in our lives, creating time the way we want it and when we want it.

Let me give you an example of making time. My first love is teaching. There have been times when I have presented over 150 classes and seminars during the course of a year. These classes and seminars took up a lot of my time, but I loved every moment of them. I have never been trained as a writer, so I find writing very demanding on my abilities. Yet I have trained myself to write by setting aside the time to write.

Because I would rather be teaching, I must make time to write. And this book was important enough for me to make that time. For three months I shut myself off from the rest of the world to complete this goal. The rest of the world and my friends thought I was dead or had disappeared! I only worked on the manuscript. After all, what are three months out of my life when the results may benefit many people?

Although I was "dead" to everyone else, I was very much alive in what I was doing. My excitement and enthusiasm were self-created and enabled me to complete the book. In essence, writing the book demanded discipline, making *time*, and creating the excitement and enthusiasm that carried me through.

So many people are bored. They say there is nothing to do. How sad this is! They drink, watch TV, play video games, cards, or bingo, and do almost anything for the sake of killing time. But while they are killing time, they are also killing their creative imaginations. They have no time for study, meditation, or self-improvement.

Life is to act. Not to act is death. The clock is ticking away. Life is an emergency. The time is now.

Visualize yourself as a person who always does things now. Everything you envision is done right away or, at the very least, you make plans to do it right away. If you really want to be emotionally strong, healthy, successful, and alive, find time to study and meditate on the principles we have been talking about. It takes time to be successful. Lots of time. There is no magic formula. It takes time, study, meditation, and action.

Make use of the time God has given you. Most people do not realize the value of time until they come to the end of it, then they beg for a few minutes more. Those who died in the last twenty-four hours would have given anything for another twenty-four hours. You can spend the next twenty-four hours reaching your true potential or sliding down into your own particular hell. The choice is always yours.

TIME BECOMES A TOOL, NOT A TYRANT

You must learn to regard the clock as an artist regards his materials. Not as a whip, but as a paintbrush to add beauty to the picture you are creating. You must be aware of the freedom of choice you are exercising and learn the value of time without fearing it. In other words, you must do whatever you do because you are using time for your purpose or objective, and in no case permit it to be an end in itself. There is no virtue in budgeting time unless you get more out of it that way.

Using time effectively depends largely upon learning to set priorities. One of the simplest but finest methods of doing this is to get into the habit of writing down each night before retiring the *six most important things you want to do the next day*. After you list these, put them in their order of priority. As you get those things done you set out to do, you will be filled with a great sense of accomplishment. Each project you complete will make the next seem easier. And success will follow success.

Allotting your hours to their best use is a splendid mental

exercise because, in so doing, you must decide on the relative importance of the items to be included in your daily activities. This type of preliminary evaluation, which helps separate essentials from nonessentials, guarantees rewards way out of proportion to the initial time involved.

The ancient Chinese proverb says, "A journey of a thousand miles begins with a single step." You must not only start moving but you must keep moving *forward*.

Managing your time efficiently does not mean you have to rush. Some people are always in a hurry but never seem to get any more done than those who pace themselves. Do you remember when you last wanted to "save time"? What did you do with the time you saved? Did you put it away to use some day when you needed it? The point is that time can be *managed* but *not saved*. Trying to save time only results in anxiety and frustration. Remember our earlier precaution: Don't save time and waste your life!

Making use of time begins with realizing how you are presently using it. Look over daily activities and see where you can make changes.

Do the most unpleasant assignments and activities first. This way, you will work harder and get more done because you will always have a pleasant task ahead.

Take time to make time. Don't forget to make time in your schedule for planning.

THERE NEVER WAS A BETTER TIME—FOR YOU

Because we exist in a universe of magnificent rhythm and timing, the body and mind respond easily to the rhythm of repetition in action. In your assumed mastery of time, never regard regularity as mundane, dull, uninteresting, or as a matter of duty. Instead, think of it as the same type of rhythm that makes music enjoyable. The challenge and invitation are to swing along with it and catch the tempo of the melody of life. One of the principal objectives of this book is to help you build more self-confidence so you can enjoy the TIME OF YOUR LIFE!

Overcoming Fear
and Worry

Fear has been around for thousands of years. Our primitive ancestors feared thunder and lightning, feared the wild beast, and feared each other. Fear was present when Noah launched his Ark. The word "fear" appears in the Bible over four hundred times. When nations are at war, the world fears an expanded conflict. When there isn't a war, we fear that there might be a war in the future. In between, we fear a thousand and one things, large and small, involving ourselves and other people and situations in our daily lives.

We were born with only two fears: the fear of falling and the fear of loud noises. The rest we developed ourselves. Fear takes many forms. There is claustrophobia, which is the fear of confined spaces; agoraphobia, the fear of open spaces; ailurophobia, the fear of cats; astraphobia, the fear of thunder and lightning; hematophobia, the fear of blood; acrophobia, the fear of heights; hydrophobia, the fear of water; nucophobia, the fear of darkness; and the worst fear of all—the fear of failure.

Fear is a destructive emotion that can deal a fatal blow to any attempt on your part to build total self-confidence. If you allow your fears to run your life, it will be impossible to create the life you truly desire.

REVERSE, NOT REHEARSE, YOUR FAILURES

By giving your *dominant thoughts* to failure, you are impelled to fail. Failure is rehearsed by constant repetition. How many times a day do you think about failing and failure? Do you ever tell people that you "know" you are going to fail? Do you find yourself thinking, "What a terrible failure I've been," or a thousand other reasons why you think you will fail? This is the kind of negative rehearsal which, when combined with early childhood conditioning, makes you respond to the greatest challenges and opportunities with, "I can't!"

What can we do to overcome our fear of failure? First, we must be willing to *face* failure. Before starting on a new endeavor, ask yourself, "What is the worst than can happen?" Be prepared mentally *should* failure occur. It is important here to distinguish this from expectation. I am not saying that you should *expect* to fail, for this would make failure certain. What I *am* saying is that if you are mentally *prepared* for the worst, you will have the confidence to enable you to meet and successfully handle even the greatest of challenges.

We worry about many things, but they all boil down to this: WE ARE NOT LIVING IN THE PRESENT MOMENT. Now think about it. You can only worry if you are either focused on the future or on the past. If you are living in the present moment, it is impossible to worry. For instance, are you worried this very

Dear Jesus,

help us to spread your presence
everywhere we go.
Flood our souls with your spirit and life.
Penetrate and possess our whole being
so utterly, that our lives may be only
a radiance of yours.

Shine through us, and be so in us,
that every person we come in contact with
may feel your presence.
Let them look up and see no longer us,
but only you!

Stay with us,
and then we shall begin to shine as you shine;
so to shine as a light to others.
The light, O Jesus, will be all from you;
none of it will be ours;
it will be you, shining on others through us.
Let us thus praise you in the way you love best
by shining on those around us.
Amen.

Blessed John Henry Cardinal Newman

second? Of course not! Why? Simply because you are reading this book and your concentration precludes worrying in the moment. The mind cannot think of two things at the same time.

Overcoming fear and worry can be accomplished by living one day at a time, or better yet, one moment at a time. Just say to yourself, "For the next few minutes, hours, or days, I will . . ." Make a positive statement and keep your promise only for that period of time. Forget about the future beyond that. If you live life a moment at a time, your worries will be cut down to nothing.

It is important to have a sense of humor. Humor is a safety valve; it keeps you from taking yourself too seriously. The problem with most people is that they take life too seriously. Even religion is too serious. What should be light, exciting, and uplifting is usually a guilt-producing experience. It goes back to what you have already learned: If you make people feel "less than" or unworthy, you can control them. It's the old situation of dependency.

But surely the Creator must have a sense of humor. If you look at the aardvark or the porcupine, it is not hard to conclude that the Creator must have a sense of humor! The Creator gave us a sense of humor to relieve our tensions. Humor allows us to laugh at our fears.

Again and again, plunge into the very thing that makes you afraid so that, in the end, your fear will be exposed for what it is—an illusion. This helps to build spiritual and emotional muscle.

Most of the time fear comes from using the mind more than the body. If you *think* too much and *neglect* action, you generate fear. Lead a more active life and you will have less time to worry. Take long walks to release body tensions. An overactive mind and an underactive body can lead to trouble. On your walk, *take this book with you*. Find a quiet spot, take a break, and without looking, open it. Your subconscious will guide you to the right spot. Read a page or two and then take the long way home. As you stride along, thinking about what you have read, your mind and body will be working in perfect *balance*. Fear starts when there is a lack of balance. The principle has been recognized in developing the body, but completely overlooked in developing the mind and bringing the two into harmony.

CHANGE, THE ORDER OF THE UNIVERSE

Mental hospitals are filled with patients who are unable to face change. These people have created ways to try and escape from it. But if there is one thing even more certain than death and taxes, it is the inevitability of change. No one can avoid it. So we must learn to accept and look forward to it.

In fact, change is what you *want*. You want beauty in life; champagne instead of beer; an automobile instead of a car; a home instead of a house. And you can only have all these things if you relinquish fear.

Change means changing your way of thinking. It also means being willing to give up things the way they are, to have them the way you want them to be! No one else can do that for you.

CHANGE COMES WITH BEING DIFFERENT

Make no mistake about it, if you are to escape from mediocrity, you must consciously decide that you *want* to be different. *All great individuals are different.* They are different from the masses. This is what makes them stand out.

You must have enough guts to say to yourself, "I will not lead a life of mediocrity. I am different. I am a fantastic person with a fantastic future. A dull life is not for me." Repeat these statements. Start right now!

If you are exhausted and fearful, perhaps there's no adventure in your life. Nothing is worse than being in a rut. To sleep in the same bed every night, eat at the same restaurants, see the same people, go the same way to work, do the same thing every day is complete madness. Sameness destroys creativity and will quickly have you banging on the psychiatrist's door. People caught up in this cycle are slaves to sameness, the ones who fear the slightest change.

When you are frustrated with your daily routine, change it. Changing does not mean disregarding others or feeling superior. It means claiming the right to speak and act for yourself and doing what is necessary to make you happy. Confucius summed it up this way: "They must often change who would be in constant happiness."

The first thing to do is to stop fighting change. Learn to live *with* it and *enjoy* it. The weather is going to change. Your company is going to change. The government is going to change. So are the people around you. Everything and everybody is going to change, so why fight it? Why not be the one who says, "Let's see what I can change to improve things."

Make the *right* changes. The right changes are always positive. Begin by changing small things every day until change becomes a way of life. Don't cling to one lifestyle. Change the furniture or your style of dress. Switch things around in your room, apartment, or house. Don't leave anything the same. Keep changing things just to make it interesting.

Do you find yourself resisting this? If you do it's because you feel threatened by change. Remember, the only way to overcome fear is to do the thing you fear the most. And if that means change, then change you must!

Change your hairdo and color. Try some new foods. If you are dissatisfied with your looks, get a makeover or consult a plastic surgeon. A new appearance may do wonders for your personality. Surprise yourself and your friends with the changed you.

Change is a habit. Your whole life is lived by habit. Since infancy, you have trained yourself to respond the way you do. Changing your life means changing your habits. Sometimes this can be unpleasant, but the process of changing a habit will only be temporary.

To overcome apprehension of change, keep in mind the ultimate *benefits* you will receive. Concentrate on the benefits instead of on the fears and assumed hardships that change might impose. Write these benefits down. Read them each day and see how the change is benefiting you.

Look at everything that comes into your life as a chance to change *for the better*. If you are about to be transferred, or if your office or department is closing down, your job position has been eliminated, your lover has left you, you have to move to a new place, or your car has finally stopped running, instead of dwelling on the negative, think of possible positive consequences. If you stop resisting, accept the change, and look forward to a new and better experience, something good will happen. Good things come when you are ready to change.

. . . .

Move Ahead Through
Positive Communication

One of the most common phrases I hear in my counseling work is, "We just don't communicate." Because most people identify communication with the written and oral word, they often feel that they are not communicating. But this is not the case at all. We are always communicating. People communicate through body language, facial expressions, gestures, mannerisms, and even silence. Our ability to communicate shows just as much in what we *don't* say as in what we *do* say.

In western culture, we do little to develop nonverbal communication. In some cultures, considerable emphasis is placed on nonverbal communication. The Japanese have a word for this: *harrigay*. Derived from two other Japanese words, *harra* meaning "stomach" and *gay* meaning "art," *harrigay* is the art of getting inside another person and trying to understand her or him with little use of the spoken word. A person is responsible not only for what he says, but for what the other person *understands* through gestures, mannerisms, expressions, body language, etc.

If you are having problems communicating with others, the first thing you must understand and accept is that *you* are responsible for others not understanding you. More than likely it is the way you come across and the way you non-verbally communicate to other people. All family problems, business communication problems, individual misunderstand-ings, and even wars are rooted in our inability to understand another's point of view. So let's begin by recognizing the fact that we cannot change others, but we *can* change our attitudes *toward* them.

Communication is a delivery system for our attitudes. The way we express ourselves is an outward manifestation of what we are thinking inside. Longfellow wrote, "A single conversa-tion across the table with a wise person is better than a ten-year study of books."

One of the greatest problems that threaten any marriage oc-curs when both partners have not learned *how* to communicate with each other. Most failures in business are not really business failures, but *people* failures. People just fail to communicate. Almost every study shows that employees view a good manager as one who can communicate with them.

Each one of us is a manager. You may be managing a busi-ness, a family, a job, an education, or a friendship. To be suc-cessful, each of these requires positive communication. Here are some ways in which you can be more effective.

LISTEN! LISTEN! LISTEN!

Nothing is more important in communications than listening. There is the old story about two women walking down a street who run into a third woman. One of the women engaged herself in conversation with the third woman for a full ten minutes. The first woman observed, while the second woman did all the talking, and the third woman did all the listening. When they finally parted, the second woman exclaimed to the first, "That's one of the most brilliant women I know!" "But," protested the first, "she hardly said a word." "I know," said the second. "But she listened. That shows she's smart!"

Developing a listening skill will prove that you, too, are smart. We all feel that anyone who has the good sense to listen to what we have to say must be a good friend. Listening has become a lost art. Notice that when you are talking most people can't wait for a pause so that they can begin talking. They really don't hear you. They are too busy rehearsing what they are going to say next.

It has been established in the study of extrasensory perception (ESP) that if you send a thought and there is no one to receive it, it simply does not exist. In other words, there has to be both a *receiver* and a *sender*. The same goes for conversation. If someone is talking to you and you are not listening, the conversation does not exist.

Listening is by far the most vital component of good communication, but it is also the most ignored. A large portion of our lives was spent in learning to read, write, and talk, but no time is spent in learning the art of listening. Most of us just want to talk, and if people don't listen, we get very upset. "Why aren't you listening?" or "You're not paying the slightest attention," we say.

Whether you are aware of this or not, the way you listen has a greater impact on others than the way you talk. The world is crying out for good listeners. Nothing threatens another person's self-esteem more than indifference. But good listening extends beyond mere silence. Signs of irritation and boredom, sarcasm, thoughtless interruptions, disagreeing with what a person is saying, and not placing any significance on what is being said all play their parts in creating gaps in our communication.

When you act this way, the other person feels rejected. Inside, he is saying, "I have something to say that's important. I need to be heard." And that person will be heard, if not by you, then by *someone else*! He will do whatever is necessary to make someone listen. The child may throw a tantrum, spill something, or fight with his brothers or sisters. The student may skip class or refuse to study. The marriage partner may use the silent treatment or stay away from home. The employee may gripe or complain. Each one will find a way to be heard.

For the most part, people do not communicate. They simply take turns talking! Many wouldn't listen at all if they didn't have to. And herein lies the problem. Few people truly want to listen or improve their listening ability.

This was proven to me a short time ago when I offered to teach two courses at a local community college. The first was on *public speaking* and the second on *listening*. Actually, I did this to prove a point. Within a few days, the speaking course was completely filled. As a matter of fact, I had to conduct two classes to accommodate the number of people that enrolled.

As for the listening course, not one person enrolled! Everyone wanted to talk, but no one wanted to listen.

If you think about it, who are the people you hold in highest esteem? They are those who will listen to you. We are attracted to people who want to hear what we have to say. This is why so many psychiatrists and psychologists have busy practices. People want someone to listen to them, even if they have to pay a hundred dollars or more per hour for the privilege.

In order to be a good listener, you must *want* to be a good listener. Each person with whom you come into contact must be made to feel important. If the head of an organization or some social or political figure whom you hold in high regard wanted to talk to you, you would be all ears. But if a street sweeper, trash collector, housekeeper, or dishwasher wanted a few minutes of your time, would you be as attentive? Probably not! Yet if all these people were to disappear for a week, who would you miss more? The important authority figures, or the people who make your life more comfortable? The point is that *all people are important* and you should let them know this by listening to them.

By wanting to be a good listener, you will find out how fascinating people are. People you may have taken for granted or considered dull and insignificant suddenly become interesting. Indeed, there are no uninteresting people; only disinterested listeners!

WE ARE MORE INTERESTED IN OURSELVES
THAN ANYONE ELSE

This is a simple fact of human nature. We have feelings, emotions, pride, and anxieties. But so does everyone else. In order to develop positive communications, we have to TAKE AN INTEREST IN OTHER PEOPLE. It is not necessary to be clever, make smart remarks, tell great stories, or prove how intelligent we are. What is necessary is that our approach be *sincere*.

Remember, communication is a two-way situation. Someone has to talk and someone has to listen. You won't be able to get people to listen unless you first get their attention. And you won't get their attention until you talk about something that interests *them*. What interests people most? Themselves! They want to discuss what *they* have done, what *they* plan to do, where *they* have been and what has happened to *them*. Never forget this!

A frequent and disastrous mistake in the art of communication is to typecast people and talk to them on that basis. Some people automatically assume that all a woman wants to discuss is home, recipes, or babies. But this is often far from the truth. Many women would prefer to talk about such diverse subjects as current events, mind power, automobiles, or vintage wines. Men, too, are assumed to have typical interests. While so-called "typical" male interests might be the stock market, football, and fishing, many would rather discuss such things as cooking, art, clothes, or self-improvement. It follows then that the smart thing to do is to try to discover the interests of the person with whom you are conversing.

Next to talking about themselves, people like to *give their opinions*. It's amusing how they will discuss things they know absolutely nothing about. Very few people will admit to not having an opinion. Rather, they will create one, right there on the spot. But while this opinion may be way off base, it is important to let them express it. You will never win a friend by disagreeing with someone's opinion.

In order of importance, the next topic people like to talk about is *other people*. They derive real pleasure from this. Sometimes what they say about others has no basis in fact but, again, they are entitled to express themselves. The trick is to point out the good qualities of the person being discussed without taking exception to what is being said. While no minds may be changed, this tactic switches the conversation to a more pleasant and positive level.

The next topic people like to discuss is *things*. They will talk about anything. Here is your chance to be a good listener and learn something. By doing just that, I have benefited greatly. Even though, initially, I may have had little interest in a subject, curiosity got the better of me and I found myself wanting to know more. By listening to people who are knowledgeable in certain areas, you can become versed in and able to converse on a surprising number of topics.

The last thing people want to talk about is . . . YOU. They don't want to hear about your sickness, your problems, or your negative views of life. Listen to yourself and note how many times you use the first-person pronoun. If it is excessive, start switching from "I" to "you"!

Keep the conversation centered on the other person. Wait until he asks about you. You can be sure that this will only be when he is ready to listen. In other words, *after* you have given him a chance to first tell you about himself. When you do talk about yourself, it should *not* be to draw attention to *you*, but to tie your interest in with those of the person with whom you are conversing.

HOLD ONLY POSITIVE CONVERSATIONS

We learned earlier that words have creative power, the same power as the thoughts that go into shaping our consciousness. As we are always communicating our thoughts, it goes without saying that these should be positive.

On those occasions when you don't feel well, avoid the tendency to complain. If you are a habitual complainer, this is your way of getting attention and sympathy. Complain often enough and you will become known as a "pain symbol" to others. They will begin to avoid you because no one wants to associate with someone who makes them feel ill. Besides affecting others, you will make yourself sicker by programming your subconscious through constant repetition. A friend of mine used to say, "Never tell anyone your troubles. Half the people don't care, and the other half are glad you have them!"

Talk about things that inspire others. Let them know how you enjoy life, and watch them respond. A person who sends out positive vibrations attracts people like a magnet.

Everyone wants to associate with those who have a happy and positive outlook because their attitude is contagious. Even if you feel down, pretend to feel good. You will uplift other people and, in the process, end up feeling better yourself.

Positive conversation also includes learning to keep secrets. You will gain the confidence of people in direct proportion to your ability to be discreet. Before disclosing something about someone else, ask yourself this question: "Would I be willing to tell this to fifty people?" Learn to say only those things you want to have repeated. If you use this approach, you will discover that your comments will automatically include only positive, constructive, optimistic observations.

USE PLAIN LANGUAGE

You simply cannot communicate with others unless you learn to use plain language. Something is definitely lacking in your ability to communicate if what you say cannot be understood by a child. Now this may sound ridiculous, but it is true. In my early years as a teacher and public speaker, I discovered that effective communication with my audience was directly related to how simple I could make complicated, abstract ideas.

The burden of holding someone's attention, whether it be an audience or an individual, falls on you. No one will pay attention to what they do not understand. Many college graduates cannot communicate with those on a lower educational level because they have never learned how to make things simple enough. If someone fails to understand you, it does not necessarily follow that they are stupid. More than likely, you have not explained your point clearly or simply enough. Walt Disney used animation as a means of simplification. Great truths are frequently told in parables or allegories. Let's learn a lesson from this and use simple stories, demonstrations, parables, and examples to convey what we mean.

One of the best methods of determining understanding is feedback. You get feedback by asking questions like these:

"Have I made myself clear?" "Do you agree?" or "What are your feelings about this?" This preliminary interchange helps develop two-way communication.

LET THE OTHER PERSON KNOW THEY ARE IMPRESSING YOU

I have already said that everyone likes to feel important. Let people know they are important by making them feel that you are impressed with what they have to say. This is done by giving your full attention to them. The less you talk about yourself, the more the other person will feel that he is important. Act as if their jobs or social lives are the most fascinating things you have heard about.

I was traveling by plane on my way home from a speech I had just given to five thousand people. I was bubbling over with excitement after an extremely successful speaking engagement. Next to me sat a man who said he was an accountant. Well, I thought, that's a comfortable profession, but how boring it must be. Of course, I didn't let him know how I felt. Instead, I listened as he talked about his travels and the complicated financial dealings of the large corporations he represented.

All the way across the country, he kept me enthralled. From this experience, a great truth emerged. Although on the surface others may appear dull, what they have to say is often more interesting and important than what we have to say ourselves.

Most people really do not communicate effectively because they are trying to *impress* rather than *express*. They engage in a sort of self-neutralizing, verbal bombardment of each other. They use words others do not understand and frequently attempt to speak down rather than *to* the person with whom they are talking. They are busy showing that person how smart they are.

Justified or not, others will form their opinions of you by the *way* you talk to them. If you show off or try to impress them with your intelligence, you can be sure that they will tune you out right away. On the other hand, if you do not talk down to them and keep their interests and emotions in mind, they will consider you clever, interesting, and even a brilliant conversationalist.

Studies have shown that 75 percent of the words you use are never heard by other people. People hear only what they want, and as you already know, the thing they most want to hear about is *themselves*. If you talk to them about their goals, interest, ideas, experiences, or aspirations, you will immediately get their attention and continue to hold it without difficulty.

GIVE SINCERE RECOGNITION

Whenever you give sincere recognition, you are, in essence, showing people how to like themselves more. If you remark about one of their attributes that escapes most people, you will increase your impact.

It takes little imagination to compliment someone on his appearance—although that's nice, too—so the creative person looks for less obvious qualities. For example, you might notice someone's sense of humor or ability to attract friends. By taking time to remark on attributes that are far too often overlooked by others, you are saying, in effect, "I really notice you as a person," thereby giving that person a reason to like him- or herself more.

By helping others build their self-esteem and making them

feel comfortable and secure, they become more relaxed and friendlier. This all goes back to what we said earlier: In order to think well of others, you must first think well of yourself. Knowing what pleases you and increases your self-confidence provides some excellent clues as to how you can make others feel self-confident. Someone observed, quite astutely, that when we look at our world and see God and good in everything and everyone, our world looks back at us with the same attitude.

WAIT UNTIL THE CONVERSATION GETS AROUND TO YOU

After others have talked about themselves, a point will be reached when the conversation will get around to you. A little patience here is well invested. Don't be like the actress I met at a Hollywood party who came up to me, talked on and on about her movie career, and finally said, "Enough about *me*! How did *you* like *my* last picture?"

ACTIONS SPEAK LOUDER THAN WORDS

What you are speaks so loudly,
I cannot hear what you are saying.
—RALPH WALDO EMERSON

People will judge you by your actions. Small acts of courtesy are not merely empty gestures; they are thoughtful expressions that say, without verbalization, "I think you are important."

Unfortunately, to many, courtesy is becoming a lost art. Don't let this happen. Be one of those people who still places importance on small acts of kindness that make others feel special.

It is important to realize that people are not interested in hearing us expound on our particular philosophy of life. They are more interested in seeing how our beliefs and philosophy are actually *working* in our life.

Your actions are reflections of your thinking. If others see that you are healthy, happy, prosperous, and enthusiastic, they will ask what you are doing to make these things happen. There is no need to "preach" because, as the saying goes, "More truth is caught than taught." Religious fanatics may talk about peace, love, salvation, and their great happiness in religion, but all one has to do is look at their lifestyles to know just how well it's working. The Bible puts it this way: "By their fruits ye shall know them." If your life is a showcase of positive living, people will want to know how they can get on the bandwagon.

BE ON TIME FOR APPOINTMENTS

Another essential aspect in the development of good personal relationships is reliability. Being on time for appointments is more important than you realize. Lateness does not merely mean that you are irresponsible, it means that you really do not care about the person you are meeting. You are, in effect, saying that that person is not important enough for you to be on time. If you had a meeting with a president or prime minister of a large country at 10:00 A.M. tomorrow morning, would you be on time? Of course you would! You would make a point of it. So, let's be honest. We can all be on time if we are *motivated*.

We violate the "on time" rule because we do not realize the consequences of our actions. "That's the way I am!" we say defiantly. But that's not the way we are. It's the way we have *chosen* to be.

Remember, then, no matter who you are meeting—executive, housewife, factory worker, secretary, salesperson, relative—or if you are attending a meeting or social gathering, *be on time*! Extend this habit to all personal relationships. Get the reputation of always being there first. If you must keep someone waiting, contact that person and explain the delay and inform him when you expect to arrive. He will admire and respect your for caring. There is nothing more upsetting and frustrating than waiting for someone who doesn't show up on time.

REMEMBER PEOPLE'S NAMES

Most of us will agree that one of the sweetest sounds is the sound of our own name. People's names are their badges of individuality, so if we remember them, we automatically win their friendship. Noting and remembering a name takes only a few minutes, but the investment of time and attention can bring rich rewards.

The principal reason why we don't remember names is that, when we are introduced, we don't really *listen* to what the other person is saying. If we recall the moment of meeting, the introduction probably sounded something like this: "Hello! My name is Mrkxgrtmp." We didn't hear the name correctly because we weren't paying attention. More than likely, our minds were on what *we* were going to say next!

To remember a name, first be sure to hear it properly. Then

make an interest-stimulating mental impression of the total person while at the same time repeating his or her name over and over in your mind. If you remember the whole person, you will remember their name.

One thing you must not do is say to yourself or others, "I have trouble remembering names." By doing so, you give your subconscious a "command," which it faithfully follows. Every time you try to remember a name, the impression is rejected because you have already stated that you cannot remember names. Refute the "command" now, and start affirming that you can remember the name of everyone you meet and recall it at will.

Remembering names should be one of the priorities on your list of self-development. *Not only will this make others feel important, it will make you more poised and self-confident.*

HOW TO MEET PEOPLE AND GET TO KNOW THEM

Don't Be Afraid to Make The First Move

Contrary to what you may believe, most people hate social gatherings. They like the idea, but dislike the prospect of meeting and mingling with strangers. If we are honest, there is not one of us who, at one time or another, hasn't felt uncomfortable at a party. The truth is that, subconsciously, we are afraid that others won't like us, and we don't want to feel rejected. It's the old need for approval springing up!

If the thought of attending a social function makes you feel uneasy at the very least, remember this: *You are not alone.*

Many feel the same way. When you accept this as the truth, you will have a lot less trouble meeting other people.

Suppose you are at a party and don't know many people. When you look around, everyone seems to be having a good time while you are just standing there wishing you were at home. But you aren't at home. And there is nothing you can do about it for the moment, so you might as well make the most of the situation.

The best thing to do is to make the first move. Select someone who is not involved in conversation and appears to be alone, and walk right up to him or her. *Assume that he or she is friendly* and act as if you expect to be both welcomed and liked. With only rare exceptions, the person will react warmly and cooperate in getting the conversation going. Having taken the initiative and broken down the barriers of shyness and timidity, you will soon find your new friend is easy to talk to.

Be friendly and let the conversation take its own course. Use the guidelines for communication set forth in this chapter. And don't try too hard. From the beginning, take for granted that that person will like you, and he will!

LEARN THE ART OF SMALL TALK

All conversations do not have to be heavy or philosophical. It is much better to start off a conversation with a stranger with "small talk." There is a very good reason for this. When you meet someone for the first time, they are wondering if you will be easy to talk to. The first things you say provide the answer and create the impression that sets the tone of the relationship. If, for example, you initiate a conversation with a question about someone's philosophy of life, they will be caught off guard and back off immediately. But if you start by asking *questions* about *them*, they will relax and the conversation will flow naturally.

If you observe television talk shows, you will notice that the host invariably starts off with simple, carefully chosen questions intended to let the guest know that the interviewer is interested in him as a person. This dispels anxiety and lets the guest talk about himself.

GET THE SMILE HABIT

A problem in communication is that people don't smile enough. Watch them on the street, at the office, or even at home. How often do they smile? Some turn a smile on and off like a light switch and use it to impress others. But their insincerity is quite obvious. A study conducted at a major university revealed that, on average, men smile at 70 percent of the women and only 12 percent of the men with whom they come in contact. This would seem to indicate that they don't care what other men think about them, but are concerned about impressing women!

Smiling is an important means of communication because it has a positive effect on others. Think how good you feel when someone smiles at you! In its simplest form, it is a way of telling you that everything's going well and that the smiler is happy to see you. Department stores have shown as much as a 20 percent increase in sales when employees smiled at customers.

People cannot help but warm up to a smiler. If you are not one, you had better get the habit right away. Smile right now!

Go ahead! Now do it again! It doesn't hurt. As a matter of fact, it makes you feel good. If there's a mirror nearby, smile and see how much better you look!

When I say that you should practice smiling in front of a mirror, I am perfectly serious. You may feel silly for a while, but as your frown and down-turned mouth disappear and you begin to radiate confidence and poise, your attitude will change. Every person is beautiful when he or she smiles.

You will *automatically* look and feel better when you smile. A smile is your way of writing your thoughts on your face! It shows that you have self-confidence. If you lack self-confidence or are consumed by unhappiness and doubt, you will have a difficult time smiling. The natural resistance to exposing your feelings to others will make your smile stiff and forced. To overcome this, get to the root of your problem and change your negative self-image.

Whenever you greet people, SMILE! SMILE! SMILE! Smile for everyone you meet. Smile for your family, friends, and co-workers. Smile for the people who frown at you. Smile in traffic. Smile on the elevator, in the store, at the bank, on the street. Smile for the janitor, the waitress, the bank teller.

Notice that I said smile FOR, not AT! The reason for this is obvious. When you smile FOR someone, you are showing sincerity. The other person will sense this and smile back. That is their way of saying, "Thanks for noticing me and making me feel important!"

Learn to want to smile and enjoy the happiness you bring into the lives of those who pass your way. Try smiling today and notice the magic it works. Remember, your smile is one of your greatest assets!

BE CAREFUL OF THE COMPANY YOU KEEP

Everyone with whom you associate affects your life. Make it a point to not only hold positive conversations, but to try as much as possible to associate with only positive people. These are the people who will inspire, motivate, and help you to live a more creative life. Negative people drain your energy with their constant putdowns and complaints about how the world has mistreated them, how their husbands or wives don't understand them, how their bosses don't value them, and how terrible they feel. Whenever possible, release these "energy vampires" from your life and seek out people who are uplifting and positive.

Achieving Total Self-Confidence Through a Positive Mental Attitude

Many people believe that a positive mental attitude is unrealistic because the positive thinker is just seeking to escape problems, tragedy, and hopelessness. But this is not the case at all. Positive thinking is a way of looking at your own problems and those of humankind and trying to solve them through constructive action. The difference between the negative and positive thinker is rather like two people's reactions to half a glass of water. The negative person says that the glass is half empty, but the positive person knows that the glass is half full.

A positive mental attitude allows you to build on your strengths and overcome your weaknesses. It helps you to realize that you were born to be great, because within you is the Power that you can use to make any dream a reality. It helps you to focus on the good things in life and allows you to give your dominant attention to what is right with you, other people, and the world. By seeing good around you, you generate a magnetism that attracts more good into your life. For, as we have noted, like attracts like.

But understand this. POSITIVE THINKING IS USELESS UNLESS IT PROMOTES POSITIVE ACTION. Thoughts or mental energy must be turned into action or kinetic energy. The kinetic energy of taking action reinforces the subconscious. And, when properly utilized, that automatic goal-producing mechanism corrects mistakes, changes courses, and brings you to your target.

POSITIVE STATEMENTS RELEASE CREATIVE POWER

The words you speak have a strong influence on your feelings, moods, personality, self-confidence, and life experience. Earlier, we pointed out how negative affirmations hypnotize us into failure, disappointment, poverty, confusion, and ill health. So what is the solution? It is not very complicated. Just apply the reverse process. Flood your mind with power words or affirmations.

The affirmations that follow declare your strengths rather than your weaknesses. They focus your mind on the positive instead of the negative, affirm what you are instead of what you are not, and affirm what you can do instead of cannot do.

Use these or similar affirmations to program your subconscious mind to create the life you desire.

MOVE AHEAD WITH THESE AFFIRMATIVE THOUGHTS

- This moment affords me infinite possibilities, for I live in the eternal now of being.

- Everything I can possibly be is right this moment a part of my consciousness.

- This moment I am prepared and equipped to accept my limitless potential.

- I am fully aware of my limitless capacity. My thinking is in the now; my vision is in the now; my anticipation is in the now.

- I choose to have my life filled with positive people.

- As I become more aware of my power to see, I am also more aware of my will to do.

- I look to no one for my desires, but recognize that everyone is a potential channel through which the Infinite can bring my desires into my life.

- I am one with Universal Mind, therefore I know what I need to know at the instant I need to know it. This knowing annihilates all ignorance from my subconscious mind.

- I am confident and efficient as I allow the Power within me to motivate and activate my consciousness.

- My actions are the logical outgrowth of this awareness. Success meets all my endeavors and I am adequate to deal with every area of my life.

- I am continually receptive to new ways and methods for my greatest good.

- I know that the creative being that I am knows how to create anything I desire.

- I am mentally and emotionally dedicated to my own good and to the good of others. I live in a friendly universe that responds to my desires and brings them into my life

- Without conceit, I can say that I am spiritually perfect. My consciousness is healthy and I enjoy it. I have no fears and no regrets. I am vitally alive right now. I am totally self-confident.

CONCENTRATE ON WHAT'S RIGHT WITH YOU

Make a list of everything that is right with you. Take a good appreciative look at it. Go over it frequently. Even memorize it. By concentrating on your assets and qualities, you will develop the inner conviction that you are a worthy, competent, unique individual. Whenever you do something right, be sure to remind yourself of it and even reward yourself for the action. In this way, you will build up a new habit pattern of concentration on what is *right* with you.

In *Alice in Wonderland*, Lewis Carroll tells us how we got the way we are and how important it is to concentrate on what is right with us.

ALICE: Where I come from, people study what they are not good at in order to be able to do what they are good at.

MAD HATTER: We go around in circles here in Wonderland, but we always end up where we started. Would you mind explaining yourself?

ALICE: Well, grown-ups tell us to find out what we did wrong, and never do it again.

MAD HATTER: That's odd! It seems to me that in order to find out about something, you have to study it. And when you study it, you should become better at it. Why should you want to be better at something and then never do it again? But please continue.

ALICE: Nobody tells us to study the *right* things we do. We're only supposed to learn from the *wrong* thing first, in order to learn what not to do. And then, by not doing what I am not supposed to do, perhaps I'll be right. But I'd rather be right the first time, wouldn't you?

There's great lesson here! Focus on what's right about your life. Keep your mind off what you don't want, but on what you do want. Remember, what we focus on, we create more of!

THE NEW YOU

As you apply the principles in this book, a successful NEW YOU will emerge:

You will be an individual of power, direction, and planned action.

You will overcome the false beliefs that have been holding you back.

You will be a friendly person who is never lonely.

You will be a self-reliant person who controls his or her own destiny.

You will not need to judge yourself or others.

You will be a poised individual with empathy for others.

You will be open and receptive to new values, concepts, and beliefs.

You will have radiant health and a longer life.

You will have a new Spiritual Awareness.

You will learn to love yourself and others more intensely than you ever have before.

A bright picture, isn't it? Sure it is, because it is a view of YOU once you have learned and applied the principles contained within these pages.

This will take a commitment to action, but it will be one of the greatest adventures of your life. Once you have committed yourself to building total self-confidence, you will never be the same again.

About Dr. Robert Anthony

Dr. Robert Anthony has been an undercover secret for some of the most successful people on the planet. For the past thirty years he has spent his life unraveling the mysteries of the mind. During that time he has earned a Ph.D. in behavioral psychology from Pacific Western University and has worked as a psychotherapist, a NLP practitioner, a master hypnotist, a personal performance trainer, and a coach.

He is licensed by the American Board of Hypnotherapy, is highly trained in all forms of Energy Therapy, and is a member of the Association for Comprehensive Energy Psychology.

Unlike most other "mind performance" and "self-improvement" experts, Dr. Anthony hasn't thrived on publicity to make a name for himself. He prefers to quietly change "one life at a time."

As a personal performance consultant, he shows his clients how to align their energy with the natural laws of the Universe—which reverses the polarity in their lives. So rather than eliminating the things they *don't* want, they become naturally attracted to the things they *do* want!

Dr. Anthony's rare "cut-to-the-chase" style makes him one of the most sought after speakers and trainers in the world.

He has lived in the United States, the United Kingdom, Sweden, Russia, and New Zealand. He currently works and lives in Australia where he runs a highly successful consulting business. He can be reached at www.drrobertanthony.com.